T three REASURE chests

*T*hree TREASURE chests

THE THREE MOST IMPORTANT THINGS IN YOUR LIFE

MITCHELL NEWPORT

Published by Three Treasure Chests Publishing and Enterprises, LLC 3TC
Mitchell.newport3tc@gmail.com

Three Treasure Chests   Special 10th Anniversary Edition Printed by Red River Print Co.,
LLC, 5300 SW 23rd Street, Oklahoma City, Oklahoma 73128, USA

Book design Copyright ©2013 and ©2024 by Mitchell Newport. All rights reserved.
Cover design and Interior design by Mitchell Newport

Published in the United States of America

ISBN: 978-1-62746-192-4

1. Religion / General
2. Religion / Christian Life / Spiritual Growth
3. Religion / Evangelism
13.10.09

"As far as lost souls, all I have to say......If this book doesn't convince them to turn their eyes upon Jesus and ask Him into their hearts...then nothing will. It's very impressive and explains salvation like I have never read before. I'll get with you next week on how many copies I need for my family and a couple of friends. I wish I could get 100! Again, I thank you for your excellent book, Mitchell! You are doing great works and I hope to see another book from Mitchell Newport!" *Terry Muncy, Mature Christian and 17 year veteran at the Headquarters of the Baptist General Convention of Oklahoma*

970-930 B.C. King Solomon Proverbs 11:30 NKJV
"The fruit of the righteous is a tree of life, And he who wins souls is wise."

"Three Treasure Chests is the very best Christian book on personal evangelism I have ever read in my entire life!" *Dr. Larry Combs, Ph.D.; Master of Sacred Literature, Old Testament and New Testament Studies; Bachelor of Religious Education and Master of Ministry, Christian Education and Pastoral Ministry; professor of Old Testament and New Testament at Crossway Bible Institute; Personal Library of over 4,000 books; Faculty AGS at Oklahoma Wesleyan University; career Baptist pastor of 35 years*

530 B.C. The Prophet Daniel Daniel 12:3 NIV
"Those who are wise will shine like the brightness of the heavens, and those who lead many to righteousness, like the stars for ever and ever."

"I am reading your book, Three Treasure Chests, right now.... WOW!.... Thank you...." *Jack Melton, messenger to Arbuckle Baptist Association* "I Finished Three Treasure Chests last night. Every non-believer needs this book. Again "WOW!" May God get the Glory.... In Christ, your brother Jack."

"I read Three Treasure Chests on Tuesday and personally led my friend to Jesus Friday!"

Three Treasure Chests is the most passionate and Biblically accurate presentation of the Gospel of Jesus Christ since Matthew, Mark, Luke and John!" *Bill Slaughter, Deacon*

33 A.D. Jesus Christ The Gospel of Matthew 28:18-20 NIV
18 Then Jesus came to them and said, "All authority in Heaven and on Earth has been given to Me. 19 Therefore go and make disciples of all nations, baptizing them in the name of the Father and of the Son and of the Holy Spirit, 20 and teaching them to obey everything I have commanded you. And surely I am with you always, to the very end of the age."

*National Christian book publisher describes Three Treasure Chests as one of the best Christian books they have **ever** published:* "Mitchell, It is my sincere honor to attach to this email our contract offer for your book, *Three Treasure Chests*. There are a few particular books in my career that I want to be known for signing. Some are known authors, some are just great stories and *then there is your book*. I want the whole world to grasp this vision from a man in Sulphur, Oklahoma. I want to be able to reach out to thousands of people to show them what we know and what God has to offer. *More so than any book I have signed I want to be known for signing the book that changed so many lives for Christ. Your book is going to be one of the most anointed and spiritually led books that we have ever done and I am so honored to be a part of this ministry*. You are a Blessing and I am so humbled by your faith and your writing. God certainly has an amazing plan for your life! We can't wait to see where this goes and we do look forward to an amazing future! *Trinity Tate-Edgerton, Executive Director Of Book Acquisitions, Tate Publishing & Enterprises, LLC*

55 A.D. The Apostle Paul 1 Corinthians 9:22 NIV
"To the weak I became weak, to win the weak. I have become all things to all people so that by all possible means I might save some. I do all this for the sake of the Gospel, that I may share in its Blessings"

Dedication

To my Heavenly Father and to my earthly dad, who became Heavenly in 1994. I love you both with all that is within me and can hardly wait to see you. I faithfully and sincerely hope and pray you are honored by these heartfelt words until then.

For every precious life and eternal soul this book and concept passionately touches, please know, as my dad and hero would so often say, "God did it."

Contents

Introduction

Three priceless treasure chests can be *yours* today. They each hold the greatest treasures you will ever know. They are by far the three most important and valuable things in *your* life. Claiming these treasures will be your crowning accomplishments of all time.

Imagine three ancient and spectacularly beautiful treasure chests displayed just for you—right now— wherever you are. Magnificent treasures overflow in all their radiant glory. *Your* name is boldly engraved on each treasure chest. God Almighty, the Creator of the universe, is lovingly offering *you* all three treasures today. You must choose to personally accept or reject the three greatest treasures of all. The wisest choice you will ever make is to read and heed these most powerful of words you now hold in your hand. These words will lead you to vast treasures beyond comprehension.

In your first treasure chest, God is offering you the greatest treasure in the entire universe: eternal life in Heaven. This is absolutely the single most important thing in your entire life. Everything you need to unlock this spectacular treasure today is found in these first three chapters. "The Greatest Story Ever Told" leads you to the greatest treasures ever known. Most never find it, yet *you* can have it *today*.

In your second treasure chest, God offers *you* the greatest treasure on the planet: abundant life on Earth. This is the second most important thing in your entire life. The seven keys found here are the only way you will ever unlock the extremely rare treasure of true abundant life on Earth, overflowing with God's many awesome blessings. Over 95 percent of people in the world never find this treasure. But 100 percent of those who read this can find it today.

In your third treasure chest, God showers you with priceless additional treasures in Heaven every time you share God's greatest treasures with others, especially your own families and friends. This is the third most important thing in your entire life. The sky is the limit for these additional treasures in Heaven. You will want to maximize these because you will get to enjoy them for all eternity!

Marvel as every page you unfold here reveals the greatest treasure map upon which your eyes will ever gaze. Seek and you will find. Your most fantastic adventure, even the greatest day of your life, is at hand.

Then when you grasp these treasures, you shall change the world.

Behold! Your quest for *Three Treasure Chests* begins right now!

The Greatest Story Ever Told

Y ou now unveil the greatest story ever told about the greatest treasures of all time, starring the greatest person who ever walked the face of the Earth! Amazingly, this divinely true tale features *you* starring in its cast. As such, it will lead *you* personally to all three treasure chests. The 788,000 most profound words throughout all history are lovingly and humbly condensed into these 3,000, just for your mind and spirit to enjoy. Please hold on tightly as I humbly strive to condense the highlights from 2,000 pages of the world's most popular study Bible into the next twelve pages just for you. So, savor each word; for the treasures the depths of your heart and soul seek most of all shall be revealed to you as never before on this extraordinary day.

From ancient origins long ago, behold the greatest story ever told!

There is only one true God. According to the Holy Bible, He is more awesome, more powerful, more magnificent, more holy, and more loving than we can imagine. God created the entire universe as we know it. He created a multitude of angels. He created Heaven and Hell. He created the Earth and all the plants and animals. "In the beginning God created the heavens and the Earth" (Genesis 1:1, niv1984). God created man in His own image. Then God created woman from the man as a suitable helper. He created them as male and female. God blessed them and said to them, "Be fruitful and increase in number; fill the Earth and subdue it" (Genesis 1:27–28, NIV1984). God gave man dominion over all the Earth and over all the animals and plants.

God gave the angels and mankind He had created their own free will. He loves us more than we can imagine. He wants us to love Him in return and serve Him and worship Him. But God does not force us to do so. He wants us to love Him and serve Him out of our own free will. God is glorified more when we honor Him freely rather than if God made us do so like robots or like puppets on a string. Ages ago, some of the angels in Heaven rebelled against God.

> And there was war in Heaven. Michael and his angels fought against the dragon, and the dragon and his angels fought back. But he was not strong enough, and they lost their place in Heaven. The great dragon was hurled down—that ancient serpent called the devil, or Satan, who leads the whole world astray. He was hurled to the Earth and his angels with him.
>
> Revelation 12:7–9 (NIV1984)

> He is filled with fury, because he knows that his time is short.
>
> Revelation 12:12 (NIV1984)

Notice that Satan and his demons are much weaker than God. In fact, it seems clear that Satan and the demons are even weaker than God's angels. "God did not spare angels when they sinned, but sent them to Hell, putting them into gloomy dungeons to be held for judgment" (2 Peter 2:4, niv1984). Satan is real. He wants to lead the whole world astray, including you and me. Clearly, though, God is destined to win. Satan is doomed to loose in the end. If you want to be on God's winning team, read on.

Mankind also rebelled against God by sinning. (You can read about Adam and Eve sinning in Genesis 3.) Besides Jesus, every person who ever lived on Earth has sinned against God, which includes you and me. The Holy Bible says, "For all have sinned and fall short of the glory of God" (Romans 3:23, niv1984). Our sins, even one sin, will keep us out of Heaven and condemn us to Hell forever unless they are forgiven by God who sees every sin. God knows every detail of every sin we have ever committed, even if nobody else in the world knows about it. "Nothing in all creation is hidden from God's sight. Everything is uncovered and laid bare before the eyes of Him to Whom we must give account" (Hebrews 4:13, niv1984).

Most people sin almost every day. There are many kinds of sins that we all need to understand. The Holy Bible clearly teaches us that sins can be actions, words, or even thoughts if they violate God's laws. Stealing or cheating in any form is a sinful action; for example, downloading free music or videos without paying the artist is stealing. Cheating on your income taxes is also sin. Using foul language or hurtful words or lying is a verbal sin. Thinking hateful or lustful thoughts about someone else are also sins according to clear teachings in the Holy Bible. (See Matthew 5.)

There are also sins of omission. If you know you should help someone and you fail to do so, that is sin. The Holy Bible tells us to take care of widows and orphans, to help the poor and needy, to feed the hungry, to visit those in prison, to work with our hands so that we can help others, to tell others about Jesus, to pray often, to study the Bible regularly, to attend church regularly, to be good examples to our children, to tithe traditionally 10 percent to God, to take good care of our bodies, to not cause another person to stumble, and so on. Every time we fail to do such things, we commit a sin of omission. For a good example, please read the parable of the Good Samaritan. Jesus Himself spoke this parable in Luke 10:25–37 about helping others in need and ended it with the command for each of us to "go and do likewise." Our sins always hurt God. They always hurt us. Our sins often hurt someone else too. Each sin damages our closeness with God. Each individual sin is enough, by itself, to keep each of us out of Heaven.

God loves you more than you can imagine. Remember, He created you in His Own image. (See Genesis 1:27.) But God also hates sin more than we know. Yes, God is a loving, caring, forgiving, and patient God Who truly wants the very best for us. But He is also a holy, righteous, and just God Who must punish our sins. God loves us and wants us to spend eternity in Heaven with Him, but He will not allow any sin to enter Heaven. God will punish all sin severely. We all sin. Our only hope is for our sins to somehow be punished and forgiven according to God's divine plan. Only Jesus offers that hope.

In the Old Testament days, more than two thousand years ago, God ordained priests to make various kinds of animal sacrifices to atone for the people's sins. The Ten Commandments and other related laws of Moses defined sin in those days. The Holy Bible says, "Without the shedding of blood there is no forgiveness of sins" (Hebrews 9:22, RSV). These animal sacrifices had to be repeated over and over again until God ultimately provided us a perfect sacrifice for our sins once and for all—Jesus Christ.

God loves us so much that He sent us a Savior, Jesus Christ, to save us from our own sins. This is God's amazing grace. God sent His Own Son, Jesus, from Heaven to take the punishment for our sins on our behalf. Jesus paid our ransom. To be saved, we must personally repent of our sins and faithfully believe in Jesus Christ as our Savior and Lord. "There is rejoicing in the presence of the angels of God over one sinner who repents" (Luke 15:10, NIV1984). Repentance means we must admit to God that we are sinners. We must ask God to forgive us; we must turn away from our sins and faithfully turn to Jesus instead as our Savior and Lord. This is God's *only* plan whereby we can have our sins forgiven. This is the only way we can ever have eternal life in Heaven. This is the only way we can ever escape an eternity in Hell. Jesus is the only key to your first treasure chest. The Holy Bible clearly tells us that *only* Jesus saves. "Salvation is found in no one else, for there is no other name under Heaven given to men by which we must be saved" (Acts 4:12, NIV1984). Only Jesus saves. Jesus Himself said, "I am the Way and the Truth and the Life. No one comes to the Father except through Me. If you really knew Me, you would know My Father as well" (John 14:6–7, NIV1984). Please never forget, *only* Jesus saves.

Many prophets in the Old Testament of the Holy Bible foretold many things about the coming Savior. Amazingly, all of these literally hundreds of prophecies would be perfectly fulfilled through Jesus Christ. God miraculously caused the virgin Mary to conceive a Son. Jesus, the Son of God, was born in Bethlehem—a small town still in modern-day Israel—approximately two thousand years ago. His birth was heralded by angels in Heaven. Poor shepherds from nearby and wealthy wise men from the Orient bearing costly gifts traveled great distances to see and worship the newborn Savior. Literally *billions* of people around the world celebrate the birth of Jesus every Christmas! It is the greatest celebration on earth! Christmas celebrates the one true Savior of the world. Only Jesus saves!

Jesus grew up as a humble carpenter. He began His public ministry at about age thirty. Jesus was God in human form. The Holy Bible clearly describes Jesus as both the Son of God and as the Son of Man. Jesus performed many miracles. He healed the sick, raised the dead, cast out demons, and preached the good news about the Kingdom of Heaven to thousands of people. This Gospel would spread to billions through today. He spoke with awesome authority about the Scriptures about having proper relationships with God and with others. Jesus knew the Scriptures very well and prayed often to His Father in Heaven. We should follow these examples Jesus set for us about devoted prayer and Bible study as we'll see in more detail.

Some of the corrupt religious leaders of the day felt threatened by Jesus. They did not recognize that Jesus was truly the Savior the prophets throughout the Old Testament had written so much about. Eventually, they schemed to have Jesus arrested and killed to selfishly protect their own prestigious positions. Jesus told His followers in advance He would shed His Own blood for our sins. He humbly, obediently, and selflessly allowed Himself to be arrested, ridiculed, falsely accused, tried and convicted, and ultimately beaten and killed by crucifixion. In this way, Jesus lovingly allowed Himself to become the One and Only perfect sacrifice for our sins. Animal sacrifices were no longer necessary. Jesus loves you and me so much that He shed His holy blood for us on the cross. Jesus became our One and Only true Savior.

If you would like to see for yourself a fairly accurate historical representation of how brutal death by crucifixion was during the Roman Empire, watch the movie *The Passion of the Christ*. (Please be aware that the realistic violence in the movie may be too graphic for younger children.) I am aware of no better visual portrayal of how much Jesus truly loves you and me. He loves each of us so much that He left His throne in Heaven and humbly allowed Himself to be crucified so that our sins might be forgiven. If you were the only sinner on earth, Jesus loved you enough to die on the cross just for you. Every person could say, "I asked Jesus how much He loved me. He answered, 'This much!' Then He stretched out His hands on the cross and died for me." Even today, contemplating "this much!" still gives me chills.

Jesus is the best friend you will ever have. Before He was crucified, Jesus said, "Greater love has no one than this, that He lay down His life for His friends" (John 15:13, niv1984). No one else will probably ever die for you, but Jesus did exactly that because He loves you so much. Jesus loves you more than you can comprehend. He left Heaven to be born in a manger. He left His throne in paradise to suffer and die for you on the cross. He died in your place to pay the penalty for your sins so you wouldn't have to yourself. He died for you on the cross so that your sins might be forgiven. He died for you so you might spend eternity in Heaven rather than eternity in Hell. "For there is one God and one Mediator between God and men, the man Christ Jesus, Who gave Himself as a ransom for all men" (1 Timothy 2:5–6, niv1984). Never forget, only Jesus saves. You are so special to God, and He loves you so much that Jesus, the King of Kings, died just for you. I love the song lyrics, "Amazing love, how can it be that You, my King, would die for me? Amazing love, I know it's true, and it's my joy to honor You. In all I do, I honor You!" ("Amazing Love" by Hillsong United) Jesus made the ultimate sacrifice because He loves you so much! Never forget how much Jesus loves you.

Please know, Jesus's love has changed me and changed my life. His profound love will change you too. Please accept Jesus's love today. You will never regret it. I rarely use the word "absolutely," but will even emphasize it here. Accepting Jesus as your personal Lord and Savior is *absolutely* the best decision of your entire life.

One of the two thieves crucified beside Jesus mocked Him. The other thief, perhaps a longtime criminal, sincerely repented and pleaded for Jesus to help him. Jesus replied, "I tell you the truth, today you will be with Me in paradise" (Luke 23:43, NIV1984). Jesus saved a convicted criminal dying on a cross. He also saved prostitutes and ruthless, thieving tax collectors who repented of their sins. God even mercifully forgave Moses, David, and the Apostle Paul after they each committed murder. Jesus wants to save you today regardless of how bad your past might be. No matter how bad your past has been, you can start a brand-new life today. Jesus loves you and will forgive you of every sin you ever committed if you will just let Him.

After Jesus died on the cross, His body was buried in a tomb. The tomb was sealed, and guards were placed there to protect it. On the third day, Jesus was raised from the dead and walked out of the tomb—just as He had predicted. The Holy Bible says,

> Why do you look for the living among the dead? He is not here; He has risen! Remember how He told you, while He was still with you in Galilee: "The Son of Man must be delivered into the hands of sinful men, be crucified and on the third day be raised again." Then they remembered His words.
>
> Luke 24:5–8 (NIV1984)

False prophets, false saviors, and false messiahs—such as Buddha, Confucius, Mohammad, Joseph Smith, David Koresch, Jim Jones, and many others like them all—remain in their graves today. Only Jesus walked out of His grave and is alive today. Only Jesus defeated death for us. Billions of people still celebrate Jesus's resurrection every Easter. At Easter, we celebrate Jesus defeating death and offering each of us eternal life in Heaven. After His resurrection, hundreds of witnesses would later see Him, talk with Him, and touch Him during the next few weeks. Thousands witnessed His many miracles before and after that very first Easter. Ultimately, Jesus ascended into Heaven in front of many witnesses.

> He was taken up before their very eyes, and a cloud hid Him from their sight. They were looking intently up into the sky as He was going, when suddenly, two men dressed in white [probably angels] stood beside them. "Men of Galilee," they said, "why do you stand here looking into the sky? This same Jesus, Who has been taken from you into Heaven, will come back in the same way you have seen Him go into Heaven"
> Acts 1:9–11 (NIV1984, commentary added)

After that first Easter, almost twenty centuries ago, Christianity spread throughout the world like wildfire. Early Christians were severely persecuted for several centuries. Yet Christianity blossomed. People realized that if thousands of Christians were willing to brutally lose their lives rather than renounce their faith, then Jesus Christ must truly be the Savior sent from God. The Holy Bible, inspired by God, recorded all of this and so much more in the greatest book in all of history.

The Holy Bible continues to proclaim Jesus Christ as our Only Savior and Lord. Jesus is our One and Only way to God. Jesus is the One and Only way to eternal life in Heaven. Therefore, Jesus is the key to your first treasure chest. Again, only Jesus saves.

You have just read "The Greatest Story Ever Told," about the greatest treasures ever offered by the greatest Person to ever walk the face of the Earth. Jesus Christ is the greatest Person to ever walk the face of the Earth. The greatest story ever told is how God loves us so much that He sent His only Son to die for us so that our sins might be forgiven. This is the only way we can become a part of God's loving family. Your first treasure chest contains God's greatest treasure: eternal life in Heaven. It is a gift from God offered to each of us. This treasure is the single most important thing in your entire life. *You* can have this treasure *today*! You hold the keys to unlock this treasure in your hands this very moment. In, perhaps, the most famous words in the entire Holy Bible, Jesus said,

> For God so loved the world that He gave His One and Only Son, that whoever believes in Him shall not perish but have Eternal Life. For God did not send His Son into the world to condemn the world, but to save the world through Him. Whoever believes in Him is not condemned, but whoever does not believe stands condemned

already because he has not believed in the name of God's One and Only Son.

John 3:16–18 (NIV1984)

Never forget: *Only* Jesus saves.

Heaven and Hell

Most people find Heaven and Hell absolutely fascinating. They are not imaginary fairy tales. Heaven and Hell are very real places whether you believe in them or not. They are as real as any place you have ever lived. Every person will spend eternity in either Heaven or Hell. That includes you and me. That includes every one of your own family members. That includes all your friends too. Once you are there, you are there forever. That's right, you will experience either Heaven or Hell for millions of years and much more. Therefore, every person would be wise to focus on eternal things much more. We should worry less about temporary things like money, jobs, careers, and material things. (See Matthew 6, entirely the words of Jesus.)

God loves you and wants you and all your loved ones in Heaven. Jesus said, "And this is the will of Him who sent Me, that I shall lose none of all that He has given Me, but raise them up at the last day" (John 6:39, niv1984). In contrast, Satan hates you and wants to deceive you into suffering an eternity in Hell under his dominion, for "he is a liar and the father of lies" (John 8:44, niv1984). When you sincerely accept Jesus as your personal Savior and Lord, you unlock the magnificent treasures found in treasure chest number one. You escape everlasting suffering in Hell. You receive God's amazing gift of eternal life in Heaven instead. God lets each person freely choose Heaven over hell. The wise do; the foolish do not. If you reject Jesus, God will reject your entry into Heaven. It's your choice. So to fully appreciate how magnificent treasure chest number one really is, we must understand a few things about Heaven and Hell.

The Holy Bible gives us a lot of very interesting details about both places. I will highlight them for you here. Heed this word of caution, though: there is a *lot* of inaccurate information floating around out there in the world about Heaven and Hell and who goes there. Please, do not believe much of what you see and hear on television, radio, movies, and in much of the print media about Heaven and Hell. Misleading information about these things is everywhere, and it is very dangerous. Many people are led astray. The most accurate information about Heaven and Hell comes to us directly from the most credible source anywhere on the subject: the Holy Bible. This chapter, and really this entire book, talks about sin and Hell, and many other vital things more frankly than what most people often hear. I do so unapologetically because people desperately need to hear the stark truth from the Holy Bible much more than our corrupted, "politically correct" society invites. Jesus said, "Then you will know the truth, and the truth will set you free" (John 8:32, NIV1984). Simply put, knowing the extremes of Heaven and Hell reveals how urgently we each need Jesus today.

So hold on for a wild ride! Here's how the Holy Bible describes Heaven and Hell!

Heaven

Heaven is a very real place. It is more magnificent, beautiful, and wonderful than our most creative minds can even imagine. The Holy Bible says, "No eye has seen, no ear has heard, no mind has conceived what God has prepared for those who love Him" (1 Corinthians 2:9, NIV1984). We will be in the very presence of God Almighty. He created the universe. He created us. He created Heaven for us. He created us for Heaven. We will have ultimate love, peace, and joy there. There will be no sorrow, pain, or tears in Heaven. We will enjoy this paradise with our family and friends who are also in Heaven forever! Heaven will be fantastic beyond our wildest dreams. Jesus said of heaven, "In my Father's house are many mansions: if it were not so, I would have told you. I go to prepare a place for you. And if I go and prepare a place for you, I will come again, and receive you unto Myself; that where I am, there ye may be also" (John 14:2–3, KJV). Jesus is lovingly preparing a Heavenly mansion for you. You can receive it today, along with many other treasures, by sincerely and faithfully receiving Him as your personal Savior and Lord.

Many places in the Holy Bible describe Heaven as awesome and magnificent in many ways. Here are a few amazing descriptions from just one passage from Revelation 21:

> Then I saw a new Heaven and a new Earth, for the first Heaven and the first Earth had passed away... I saw [Heaven] prepared as a bride beautifully dressed for her husband. And I

heard a loud voice from the throne saying, 'Now the dwelling of God is with men, and He will live with them. They will be His people, and God Himself will be with them and be their God. He will wipe every tear from their eyes. There will be no more death or mourning or crying or pain, for the old order of things has passed away…. It shone with the glory of God, and its brilliance was like that of a very precious jewel, like a jasper, clear as crystal. It had a great, high wall with twelve gates, and with twelve angels at the gates….The wall was made of jasper, and the city of pure gold, as pure as glass. The foundations of the city walls were decorated with every kind of precious stone…. The twelve gates were twelve pearls, each gate made of a single pearl. The great street of the city was of pure gold, like transparent glass. I did not see a temple in the city, because the Lord God Almighty and the Lamb [Jesus] are its temple. The city does not need the sun or the moon to shine on it, for the glory of God gives it light, and the Lamb is its lamp. The nations will walk by its light, and the kings of the Earth will bring their splendor into it. On no day will its gates ever be shut, for there will be no night there. The glory and honor of the nations will be brought into it. Nothing impure will ever enter it, nor will anyone who does what is shameful or deceitful, but only those whose names are written in the Lamb's book of life.

Revelation 21:1–27
(NIV1984, comment added)

The day you are saved, unlocking treasure chest number one, your name is engraved in the Lamb's Book of Life. Jesus said, "Rejoice that your names are written in Heaven" (Luke 10:20, NIV1984). These vast, magnificent treasures await you!

We can faithfully trust that God makes special provisions for young children to go to Heaven who are not yet old enough to be accountable for their own salvation. Jesus once called a little child and had him stand among them. Jesus then said, "I tell you the truth, unless you change and become like little children, you will never enter the Kingdom of Heaven. Therefore, whoever humbles himself like this child is the greatest in the Kingdom of Heaven" (Matthew 18:3–4, NIV1984).

Heaven is more spectacular than all the greatest sights on earth combined. Now, focus like a laser right here. If we could spend just one day in Heaven, we would be so transformed by its amazing love and beauty and majesty that we would devote the rest of our lives to passionately urging everyone we know to get right with God and make Heaven their eternal home. So, out of sincere love, I *passionately* urge you to do so today! In fact, I beg of you, as desperately and lovingly as I know how, to please choose Heaven over Hell today before it's too late. This book is a perfect tool to encourage those you know and love to choose Heaven over Hell while there is still time.

Treasure chest number one contains, among other fantastic treasures, your personal ticket to Heaven for all eternity! It is your choice whether to claim your free ticket to Heaven or not. Please do so. You will never regret it. Sincerely, from the bottom of my heart, helping as many people as possible get to Heaven is what motivates me to write every word here. If we truly love God and love others, we will do everything possible to help others get to Heaven. An expert in the law asked Jesus,

> "Teacher, which is the greatest commandment in the Law?" Jesus replied: "Love the Lord your God with all your heart and with all your soul and with all your mind. This is the first and greatest commandment. And the second is like it: Love your neighbor as yourself. All the Law and the Prophets hang on these two commandments."
>
> Matthew 22:35–40 (NIV1984)

These are the two "greatest commandments" in the Holy Bible. In that profound light, if we truly love God and love others, we will do everything possible to help others get to Heaven. Please give your family and friends copies of this book. Lovingly urge them to simply read it and heed it. It is very likely the best invitation to Heaven they will ever see. What better way to love God and love others with such a thoughtful gesture. Please share God's greatest treasures with all those around you.

Think of at least the thirty, sixty, or one hundred–plus people you care about most. These family members, friends, coworkers, and others you encounter every day form your very unique sphere of influence. Make it your mission in life to share all the treasures in this book with everyone in your personal sphere of influence as soon as you possibly can. This is the most loving thing you can do for them. Prepare to be fascinated in a few pages by the numbers thirty, sixty and one hundred—God's numbers, not mine.

Hell

Hell is a very real place too. The Holy Bible repeatedly describes Hell as a *horrible* place of eternal suffering, torment, hopelessness, fire, thirst, agony, and even weeping and gnashing of teeth. (See Matthew 8:12; Luke 16:19–31; and Revelation 20:10 for a few examples.) You don't have to trust me on this, just trust the Holy Bible—Hell is a *terrible* place. Please, focus like a laser one more time here. If we could spend just one day in Hell, we would be so terrified by the experience we would spend the rest of our lives passionately warning our loved ones and everyone we know. So, I am lovingly warning you right now to the best of my ability. People in Hell are also desperately trying to warn us right now. Jesus Himself tells us the fascinating yet frightening story of two men who died. One man goes to Heaven and the other to Hell.

Here is how Jesus Himself dramatically described it:

> There was a rich man who was dressed in purple and fine linen and lived in luxury every day. At his gate was laid a beggar named Lazarus, covered with sores and longing to eat what fell from the rich man's table. Even the dogs came and licked his sores.

The time came when the beggar died and the angels carried him to Abraham's side [in Heaven.] The rich man also died and was buried. In Hell, where he [the rich man] was in torment, he looked up and saw Abraham far away, with Lazarus by his side. So he called to him, "Father Abraham, have pity on me and send Lazarus to dip the tip of his finger in water and cool my tongue, because I am in agony in this fire."

But Abraham replied, "Son, remember that in your lifetime you received your good things, while Lazarus received bad things, but now he is comforted here and you are in agony. And besides all this, between us and you a great chasm has been fixed, so that those who want to go from here to you cannot, nor can anyone cross over from there to us."

He answered, "Then I beg you, father, send Lazarus to my father's house, for I have five brothers. Let him warn them, so that they will not also come to this place of torment."

Abraham replied, "They have Moses and the Prophets [a reference to Biblical scriptures]; let them listen to them."

"No, father Abraham," he said, "but if someone from the dead goes to them, they will repent."

He said to him, "If they do not listen to Moses and the Prophets [the scriptures], they will not be convinced even if someone rises from the dead."

Luke 16:19–31 (NIV1984)
[commentary/clarification]

Of course, poignantly, Jesus Himself would soon rise from the dead that first Easter morning not long after He told this very story!

In this dramatic description that Jesus so eloquently gives us, the rich man's desperate pleas from Hell for himself and his family were in vain. The man tragically admits he is in agony in Hell. Abraham agrees the man is in agony. Once you find yourself in Hell, you can never get to Heaven. You can never again warn your loved ones. There are no second chances (as Hollywood so often portrays so inaccurately). All hope is lost. Part of your everlasting torture in Hell may be regretfully remembering how these very words pleaded with you to choose Heaven instead of Hell today before it was too late.

Part of your torment in Hell will be in knowing you will never have another chance to warn any of your family and friends. Warning your family and friends today is the greatest and most loving thing you will ever do for them. The moment we die, it is forever too late to change our minds. Our eternal fate is decided. The Holy Bible explains, "Just as man is destined to die once, and after that to face judgment, so Christ was sacrificed once to take away the sins of many people" (Hebrews 9:27–28). None of us knows exactly when we will die and face judgment before God. Thousands die unexpectedly each and every day. Please, get right with God right now, before it's forever too late. Please warn all of your own family and friends now, not later! Tomorrow may be too late! This book is entirely designed as a perfect tool to easily, accurately, thoroughly, and effectively warn others in a loving and purely Biblical manner before it's eternally too late. Please lovingly give your family and friends a copy as soon as you can if you truly love them and want what is best for them.

More specifically, please warn at least the thirty, sixty or one hundred–plus people closest to you in your own personal sphere of influence about the horrors of Hell as soon as you possibly can. As you will see in the Great Commission, Jesus used these very numbers thirty, sixty, and one hundred in this precise context.

Hell is not a big party with your friends. Hell is not silly Halloween costumes. Hell is not eternal sleep. Hell is not a fairy tale. Nothing about Hell is funny. Most television shows and movies portray Hell incorrectly. Many lies and jokes about Hell were diabolically created by Satan to trick millions of people into not taking Hell seriously. The Holy Bible teaches and warns us that Hell is very real. I will now repeat myself for emphasis here; Hell is a terrible, horrible place of eternal suffering, torment, hopelessness, agony, and pain. You should not wish Hell on even your worst enemies. You should pray for their eternal souls. God loves us and wants every person to repent of their sins and be saved from an eternity in Hell by trusting Jesus. Likewise, we should love others enough to warn them today. God wants you to choose Heaven over Hell. I beg of you as desperately and lovingly as I know how: *please* choose Heaven over Hell today before it's too late. The only key to escape Hell is in your hand right now. Please sincerely pray the prayer on page 44 as soon as you can. Please, urgently encourage your own friends and family to do the same to the best of your ability.

Every person has sinned against God and therefore does not *deserve* to go to Heaven. Romans 3:23 says, "For all have sinned and fall short of the glory of God" (NIV1984). Romans 6:23 goes on to explain, "For the wages of sin is death, but the gift of God is eternal life in Christ Jesus our Lord" (NIV1984). Our sins will lead each of us directly to death and Hell forever unless we choose to receive the free gift of eternal life in Heaven which God so graciously offers us. Sincerely helping as many people as possible to avoid Hell is also what motivates me to write these words.

Did you know that, tragically, most people who die go to Hell, not Heaven? The Holy Bible itself and modern statistics both confirm this fact. Please, I urge you, don't be one of them. This is very scary stuff. Jesus gives us this exact warning when he urges us to "enter through the narrow gate. For wide is the gate and broad is the road that leads to destruction, and many enter through it. But small is the gate and narrow is the road that leads to life, and only a *few* find it" (Matthew 7:13–4, NIV, emphasis added). The Holy Bible, Jesus's own words, tells us that this very moment many people are speeding along the broad road to Hell. Only a few are on the narrow road that leads to eternal life in Heaven. Which road are you on today? Please, get on the right road right now before it's too late! Please, get your family and friends on the right road too.

Jesus's words remain true, even two thousand years later. Many are headed for hell. Few are headed for

Heaven. Yet Hollywood and much of the mass media often tend to imply just the opposite. This gives many people a false sense of security about eternity. Satan loves this deception. Satan may directly cause this deception himself. He certainly encourages it and takes advantage of it. Consider these chilling facts: Of the 8 billion people alive in the world today, only about one-third even claim to be Christians. Research consistently indicates that some who *claim* to be Christians really have never personally repented of their sins and received the gift of eternal life as God requires in the Holy Bible. They have never accepted Jesus Christ as their personal Lord and Savior. By some estimates, over 75 percent of the people in the world are not truly Christians headed for Heaven when they die. Bluntly stated, over 75 percent of people worldwide likely go to Hell after they die. Due to Satan's many deceptions and distractions, millions in today's hectic culture do not even realize they are speeding down the wrong road in the wrong direction. Heed Jesus's warning.

Please help me warn the millions going the wrong way by warning those closest to you first. By all means, if you suspect someone is going the wrong way, make absolutely sure you are not traveling the same direction.

Here are some alarmingly tragic numbers. Statistically, about 153,000 people die worldwide every day—on average. Sadly, less than 25 percent of them likely enter Heaven. That means an estimated 1.3 persons per second enter Hell. More than 80 people per minute enter Hell. More than 4,800 people per hour enter Hell. More than 114,000 people per day hopelessly begin eternity in Hell. Please don't be one of them. Please don't let any of your family and friends be one of them. Today over 114,000 people, who are not that different from you or me, waited one day too long to get right with God. Those shocking numbers cry out for every single Christian to *immediately* and passionately tell every one they know the one true way to escape Hell. Today, you can wisely change the road you are on. Please do so wherever you are. Please do so right now. Please warn others. Please give your loved ones a copy of this book as fair warning—probably the best warning they will ever see. By that simple yet profound act of love you can heroically help save their eternal soul. Yes, *you* are eternally their hero.

Do you know, with 100 percent certainty, that if you died this minute, you would spend eternity in Heaven and not in Hell? Most people are not 100 percent sure. You can be 100 percent sure today. The Holy Bible says, "I write these things to you who believe in the name of the Son of God so that you may *know* that you have eternal life" (1 John 5:13, NIV1984, emphasis added). God wants you to choose Heaven over Hell right now, once and for all. Can't you feel God's love gently whispering to your soul right now that you want Heaven, not Hell, to be your eternal home? You can know today, 100 percent for sure, that Heaven will be your eternal home according to the Holy Bible. Please, be sure. Eternity is way too long to get it wrong.

Most people today simply do not accurately know who goes to Heaven and who goes to Hell according to the Holy Bible. For many reasons, most simply do not know the most fundamental Biblical truth about faithfully trusting Jesus for salvation. Satan loves this confusion. He deceives millions into trusting any other false path. We've just learned God's one true path to Heaven: Faithfully trusting Jesus as your personal Savior and Lord and repenting of your sins. Still, out of an abundance of caution, let me clarify some things here (even some otherwise good things) the Holy Bible clearly teaches us that will never get you to Heaven.

Fourteen Things That *Don't* Lead to Heaven

1. Being a good person.
2. Doing more good things than bad.
3. Doing lots of charity work.
4. Doing lots of religious things.
5. Regular or even perfect church attendance.
6. Church membership.
7. We can *never* earn or deserve heaven by our own efforts.
8. Following the Ten Commandments.
9. Baptism alone (without the underlying repentance and saving faith in Jesus it beautifully symbolizes).
10. Religious training or education alone.
11. Simply believing God exists does not save a person from Hell. This surprises many people. The Holy Bible says, "You believe that there is one God, Good! Even the demons believe that and shudder" (James 2:19, niv1984). To be saved one must go

farther than the demons and repent and faithfully trust Jesus as their personal Savior and Lord.

12. Believing God wouldn't send people to Hell is no excuse. Our own unforgiven sins send us to Hell. It's our own fault, not God's, if we reject Jesus until we die. Here's a simple analogy. It is the drug dealer's fault he is in jail for his crimes. It's not the judge's fault for sentencing him to jail. Anyone in Hell has only themselves to blame.

13. Certainly, *no* path to Heaven exists through Satanism, witchcraft, voodoo, and the many other forms of the occult increasingly infecting our bookstores and social media like a cancer. The Holy Bible clearly and specifically prohibits them:

> Let no one be found among you who sacrifices his son or daughter in the fire, who practices divination or sorcery, interprets omens, engages in witchcraft, or casts spells, or who is a medium or spiritist or who consults the dead. Anyone who does these things is detestable to the Lord.

> Deuteronomy 18:10–12 (NIV1984)

Throw away or destroy any tarot cards, Ouija boards, or other occult related things you have. They are not games. They are perilous gateways to allow Satan to creep into your life and destroy your family. Please, don't even read horoscopes. In fact, I pray all Christians would urge their local newspapers to permanently remove horoscopes from their pages. Avoid psychics, mediums, spiritists on TV, the internet, on social media, and in our communities. Stay far away from such things that God detests. Also, never believe any dangerous lies that suggest Satan, demons, and/or Hell do not exist at all. God's truth in the Holy Bible says just the opposite. Believe God's word, not Satan's lies.

14. Religious cults, false religions or other belief systems whose doctrines and beliefs seriously differ from true Biblical Christianity are not safe paths to Heaven. Beware! They will often try to deceive you otherwise. My purpose here is not to opine whether any particular organization is or is not a cult, but, more fundamentally, to simply and lovingly warn you of eternally dangerous doctrines. Doctrinal comparisons can be very complex and go well beyond the scope of this book. However, the Christian reference book entitled *The Kingdom of the Cults* by Walter Martin is considered by many the definitive work on the subject of cults and other religious entities. It thoroughly analyzes, compares, and contrasts each belief system with the central beliefs of true Biblical Christianity. The most recent edition of *The Kingdom of the Cults* identifies the following entities as spiritually dangerous non-Christian cults, religions or other belief systems that stray so far from true Biblical Christianity that no one should trust them with their eternal soul:

- Jehovah's Witnesses (the Watchtower Bible and Tract Society)
- Mormonism (Church of Jesus Christ of Latter-Day Saints)
- Christian Science (First Church of Christ, Scientists)

- the Theosophical Society
- Buddhism
- Baha'i Faith
- New Age Cults
- the Unification Church (the Moonies)
- Scientology (Dianetics)
- Rajneeshism
- ISKCON or International Society for Krishna Consciousness (Hare Krishnas)
- Hinduism
- Transcendental Meditation
- World Faith Movement
- Apocalyptic Cults
- Islam
- Unitarian-Universalism.

If you or anyone you know is involved with any of these entities listed above, please be warned. Do not trust any literature or other materials from these groups. Trust only the Holy Bible. You would be wise to carefully read all the introductory chapters of *The Kingdom of the Cults* as well as the chapter dedicated to that particular dangerous cult or corrupted belief system. I've personally used exactly this to lovingly help rescue precious souls and families from them. Should any organization discourage your scrutiny, recognize that as another clear warning sign to you. If you prayerfully, honestly, and sincerely seek God's truth, He will lead you in the way you should go. Remember, it is your eternal soul hanging in the balance today. Realize your children's souls may follow. Many children are chained to these eternally perilous entities. Please, break the chains that hold you in bondage. Free yourself. Then help free your parents and others you love.

Please understand, this information is not meant to offend or embarrass anyone from these other belief systems. However, as devoted Christians, we should sincerely love God and love others enough to humbly, accurately, and thoroughly share true Biblical Christianity with them in a compassionate and loving manner. We should similarly share Christian truth with those of the Jewish faith who do not believe Jesus is the Messiah, Son of God, Savior, and Lord regardless of their adherence to other portions of the Holy Bible.

Since the Tower of Babel, man keeps trying to dream up shortcuts to Heaven like we've just seen. Many of these futile efforts involve man pridefully trying to save himself in various ways or earn or deserve Heaven by his own efforts. For true salvation, we must never *pridefully* trust in ourselves; rather, we must *humbly* trust in what Jesus did for us on the cross and through His divine resurrection.

Simply remember, only Jesus saves. Nothing else can save you from Hell.

I heard an interesting little story years ago. It would be somewhat amusing but for the fact it illustrates another way many people are deceived into an eternity in Hell apart from God, rather than an eternity in Heaven with God. The story goes something like this:

> Satan gathered all his demons together for a strategy meeting. He asked his devilish

underlings for ideas to keep more people from becoming Christians. Various demons shouted out numerous worldly temptations such as drugs, materialism, illicit sex, power, selfish-ness, greed, cults, and various forms of the occult that could be used. But Satan was most interested in what a little, soft-spoken demon over in the corner had to say. The little demon suggested to Satan, "Don't tell people not to get saved. Just tell them to *wait*. Millions will wait until it's too late." Satan has had great diabolical success with this strategy ever since.

Don't stay in Satan's procrastination cult another day. Never forget about the extremes of Heaven and Hell. Understanding them better should motivate us to act as quickly as we can. Don't wait. Doing nothing today thrills Satan. Don't play Russian roulette with your eternal soul even one more day. Waiting another day to get right with God is playing with fire—literally Hell fire.

Here is ultimate wisdom: choose Heaven over Hell today.

Here is ultimate love and wisdom: help others choose Heaven over Hell today.

Finding and Unlocking
Treasure Chest Number One:

Eternal Life in Heaven

I faithfully and prayerfully trust that God is lovingly speaking to your heart, mind, and soul this very moment. God is inviting you into His family. He is offering you the free gift of eternal life in Heaven and a wealth of other awesome treasures. Search your heart, mind and soul right now. Deep down, don't you feel a desire to get right with God once and for all and make Heaven your eternal home? That deep desire in your heart is God lovingly speaking to you, inviting you into His wonderful family. God wants you to come closer to Him and share His wonderful love. Please, join God's family right now, wherever you are. Please, don't be deceived by Satan who, this very minute, might be tempting you to wait or procrastinate or get distracted until it is finally too late for you. Trust God's word in the Holy Bible to strengthen you this second. "I tell you, now is the time of God's favor, *now* is the day of salvation" (2 Corinthians 6:2, NIV1984, emphasis added).

Jesus is lovingly knocking on the door of your heart. Jesus said, "Those whom I love I rebuke and discipline.

So be earnest, and repent. Here I am! I stand at the door and knock. If anyone hears My voice and opens the door, I will come in" (Revelation 3:19-20, NIV1984). Please, repent and let Him in right now. Please invite Jesus into your heart this very moment.

Below is the key for you to unlock the ultimate treasure chest right now: God's free gift of eternal life.

As honestly and sincerely as you can, slowly pray this prayer to God. Think about every word and truly mean it. God loves you. God wants to save you right now. He is listening to you right now. God knows your every thought. This is just between you and God. Wherever you are right now, please pray:

> Dear God, my Heavenly Father, I humble myself before You right now. I believe You are the one true almighty, holy, righteous, and loving God. You alone deserve my most sincere love, honor, respect, and worship. I repent of all my sins. I admit that I am a sinner. I am sorry that my sins have hurt You, others, and myself. I realize there is no way I can ever save myself from my own sins. I cannot undo my sins by any of my own actions or good works. I realize that because I have sinned against You, as Almighty and Holy God, You have every right to justly exclude me from Heaven forever. I know I do not deserve to be forgiven. Because of my sins, I deserve Hell, not Heaven. But because of Your wonderful grace and love, You have offered me a way to have my sins forgiven through faith in Your Son, Jesus Christ. I accept Your amazing grace right now. By faith, I believe

Jesus Christ is Who the Holy Bible says He is. Jesus performed many miracles and taught us truth about God. He died on the cross for me so that my sins could be forgiven. I believe Jesus Christ was resurrected on Easter morning and later ascended into Heaven with You, God, our Heavenly Father. I believe Jesus is living in Heaven with You right now. I believe You are preparing a wonderful place for me and for all other Christians to live forever in Heaven with You. I pray for Jesus to come into my heart and save my eternal soul right now. I desire for Jesus Christ to be my Savior from all my sins. I desire for Jesus Christ to be Lord of every aspect of my life from now on. I believe You know what is best for my life. Please help me to become the person You want me to be. Help me to serve You every day of my life from now on. I want to serve You because You deserve my service since You are God Almighty. You created me to serve You. It is the greatest privilege in life to serve You. I look forward to my exciting new life as a born-again Christian. I also want to serve You to thank You for saving me. Thank You for hearing my prayer. Thank You for forgiving my sins. Thank You for accepting me into the loving family of God. Thank You for saving me from my sins and from an eternity in Hell. Thank You for giving me the gift of eternal life in Heaven: the greatest treasure of all. Amen.

_____ _____
Signature/Date

If you just sincerely prayed this prayer, let me be the first to congratulate you! Today is the first day of the rest of your amazing new and eternal life as a Christian!

> Please sign your name and the date you prayed this most important of all prayers. Keep and treasure this signed and dated copy for posterity. Show it to your children and grandchildren. Your Godly example will be very powerful to them. Eventually, you can pass it down to them as a great legacy from you. We would love to hear of your decision and celebrate with you. Each soul saved is a great victory that inspires and encourages us.

Jesus said there is great rejoicing in Heaven when even one sinner repents. (See Luke 15:7.) Welcome to the family of God! Many are rejoicing with you. You are now spiritually born-again as a child of God into God's very own loving family! You are now a Christian with Jesus Christ as your personal Savior and Lord! God's Holy Spirit now lives inside you! God is with you wherever you go! For the first time in your life, you no longer have to fear death and an eternity in Hell! You can look forward to spending eternity in Heaven with God and with all other Christians throughout history! God will not tell you one day, "I never knew you. Away from me, you evil doers" (Matthew 7:23, NIV1984)! Instead, you can look forward to God *welcoming* you into Heaven with the words, "Well done, good and faithful servant"(Matthew 25:21, NIV1984)!

You now have millions of brand-new Christian brothers and sisters who love you! (Well, there are a few really grumpy ones too, but we'll just let them be for now.) You can also look forward to starting a wonderful, exciting, and challenging new life as a Christian! The Christian life is the best life you can possibly have on Earth! We'll look more closely at that in the next chapter. Encourage your family and friends to invite Jesus into their hearts, too.

The moment you became a Christian, you accomplished something far more important than anything else in the world. Becoming a Christian is more important than becoming the president of the United States. It is more important than becoming a king or queen. Becoming a Christian is more important than discovering a cure for cancer or walking on the moon. It is more important than inventing the light bulb or the printing press or the computer. Becoming a Christian is much more important than being *financially* rich or famous or powerful by worldly standards. Instead, you have the unequaled, everlasting riches of Heaven. (See Ephesians 2:6–7.) You have the fame of having your name engraved in the Book of Life in Heaven beside all the greatest characters in the Holy Bible, who will become your friends forever. (See Revelation 3:5 and 20:11–15.) You have the awesome, unlimited wisdom and power of God at your disposal! (See James 5:16.) Becoming a Christian is more important than building the pyramids in Egypt, the Great Wall of China, or the space shuttle. Almost all accomplishments on Earth are temporary and eventually fade away or are forgotten with time. Even the pyramids will one day erode back into sands in the desert. Eternal life in Heaven lasts for all eternity. Priceless!

Change the World

Becoming a Christian is also the best way for anyone to make the world a better place, even before we get to Heaven. Most people would love to change the world. They just don't know how. If you want to really change the world for the better, becoming a Christian is your very best first step. You immediately reduce Satan's kingdom and negative, sinful influence in the world by one life: yours. At the same time, you increase the kingdom of God and positive Christian influence in the world by one life. Now your life, divinely empowered by God, will help spread God's love in the world. During the rest of your life, your Christian influence on the people and the world around you will make the world a better place day by day. God's love, peace, goodwill, and compassion will multiply through you and others you know. Shine God's radiant light and love to all within your own special sphere of influence. God will honor your Christian influence and will bless you and those around you in countless ways. So if you really want to change the world for the better, becoming a Christian is the best way to do it. The second best way to make the world a better place then is to help others become Christians too. You are about to learn the easiest, best way to do that as well! You hold in your hands the very best way to change the world for the better.

Most of the problems and social ills in our world are caused by and aggravated by sin. Sin is the real culprit. Various social problems are only the result. Sin is the disease. Social illnesses are only the *symptoms*. Non-Christian efforts and most political plans to solve the world's problems typically only treat the *symptoms* of sin. They don't treat the disease itself. It is like putting a Band-Aid on a bullet wound. It is like only treating a malignant cancer with aspirin. The pain might lessen temporarily, but the disease remains and gets worse. Becoming a Christian and living a Christian life effectively treats the *entire* disease of sin in our world, rather than just temporarily numbing the symptoms. It is like surgically removing the entire cancerous tumor. It effectively begins curing both the disease and all the symptoms better than anything else at the same time. This is why becoming a Christian, and then helping others do so, are your best first steps to really making the world a much better place. God empowers faithful Christians to change the world in ways that governments, secular organizations, and non-Christian charities cannot do without God's divine love and wisdom. So from this day forward, let us be doers of God's word and not merely hearers only. (See James 1:22–25.)

Becoming a Christian is the best thing you could ever do for your *spouse*. Many spouses eventually become Christians after months or even years of watching their spouse live a devoted Christian life. "For the unbelieving husband has been sanctified through his wife, and the unbelieving wife has been sanctified through her believing husband" (1 Corinthians 7:14, NIV1984). Just be patient, loving and kind, not judgmental. Be a good example. Of course, if you are not yet married, make it a priority to ensure both you and your spouse to be are already sincere Christians before your wedding. God instituted marriage as a wonderful three-way covenant between God, the husband and the wife. The very best marriages are between two committed Christian spouses with God prioritized at the center of the family.

Becoming a Christian is the best thing you could ever do for your *children*. Every loving parent should want their kids to be raised with sincere, moral, Biblical values, around loving and devoted Christian friends. All parents should make sure it is their number one priority in life to ensure their children are raised in a loving Christian home and encouraged to trust Jesus at appropriate ages. Every loving parent should desire, more than anything else, to ultimately enjoy eternity in Heaven with all of your children. Please, lovingly share all three treasure chests with all your children and grandchildren. This is your greatest legacy to them.

Similarly, becoming a Christian is also the best thing you could ever do for all of your family and friends. As a devoted Christian, you will become a better friend to others. You will become a better family member. As a Christian, you will develop Godly, agape love for others. Agape love is the greatest type of love of all. It selflessly gives to others, expecting nothing in return. That's how Jesus loved us on the cross. As you grow and mature in love, compassion, patience, humility, and forgiveness of others you become more like Jesus every day. He perfectly demonstrated all these and more for us to follow. Anyone who truly cares about you and loves you will be extremely proud and excited that you have become a Christian. Your relationships with family and friends can finally become all God wants them to be. You can expect some of your most important relationships to improve considerably. Some may blossom like never before.

The day you become a Christian is the greatest day of your life. That day is the first day of the rest of your eternal life. Welcome to the family of God! I'm thrilled to be your brother!

Now, let's see how you can have the very best life possible on Earth even *before* you get to Heaven!

Finding and Unlocking Treasure Chest Number Two

Abundant Life on Earth

You now know treasure chest number one contains the greatest treasure in the universe, including eternal life in Heaven. Remember, it is first on the list of the three most important things in your life.

Now it is time to move on to treasure chest number two. Treasure chest number two contains the greatest treasures on Earth. We will refer to this treasure as "abundant life on Earth." Abundant life is the absolute best life possible on Earth until the day we get to Heaven. It is second on the list of the three most important things in your life.

God wants you to have the best of both worlds, Heaven and Earth. He created both of them for you. He created you for both of them. God wants you to have the most abundant life here on Earth and then a fantastic eternal life in Heaven beyond your wildest imaginations!

Behold! Your quest for your second treasure chest—abundant life on earth—begins here and now!

Abundant Life on Earth

God wants to give you the best life possible while you are here on Earth. The Holy Bible calls this an abundant life. Jesus said, "I am come that they might have life, and that they might have it more *abundantly*" (John 10:10, KJV; emphases added).

The Holy Bible repeatedly makes it clear we can have an abundant life on Earth, even before we get to Heaven. We just need to be wise enough to do things God's way, not our own often selfish or corrupt way. "The Lord will grant you *abundant* prosperity—in the fruit of your womb, the young of your livestock and the crops of your ground" (Deuteronomy 28:11, NIV; emphases added). "You brought us to a place of *abundance*" (Psalm 66:12, NIV; emphases added). "I will bless her with *abundant* provisions" (Psalm 132:15, NIV; emphasis added). "All nations on Earth...will be in awe and will tremble at the *abundant* prosperity and peace I provide" (Jeremiah 33:9, NIV; emphases added). "For everyone who has will be given more, and he will have an *abundance*" (Matthew 25:29, NIV; emphases added). "How much more will those who receive God's *abundant* provision of grace and the gift of righteousness reign in life through the one man, Jesus Christ" (Romans 5:17, NIV; emphases added). "To God's elect...who have been chosen according to the foreknowledge of God the Father, through the sanctifying work of the Spirit, for obedience to Jesus Christ and sprinkling by His blood: Grace and peace be yours in *abundance*" (1 Peter 1:1–2, NIV; emphases added). "To those who have been called, who are loved by God the Father and kept by Jesus Christ: Mercy, peace and love be yours in *abundance*" (Jude 1:2, NIV; emphases added). Jesus said, "The knowledge of the secrets of the Kingdom of Heaven has been given to you, but not to them. Whoever has will be given more, and he will have an *abundance*. Whoever does not have, even what he has will be taken from him" (Matthew 13:11–12, NIV; emphases added).

Everyone wants to have the most abundant life possible here on earth. However, most people's lives could be much better. Why? Here's the answer: Most people try in vain to improve their lives primarily through their own efforts. Trust me here—or at least trust the Holy Bible—God can make your life here on earth *much* better than you ever could yourself through your own efforts. He created you. He created the world you live in and everything around you. God knows better than you what you really need in your life. Jesus said, "Your Father knows what you need before you ask Him" (Matthew 6:8, NIV1984). God can give you true peace, joy, fulfillment, and purpose much better than you can on your own.

Imagine that treasure chest number two is sitting in front of you right now. It contains your most abundant life on Earth. Your second treasure chest has seven individual locks on it. Each lock requires a different key. I am about to give you all seven keys to unlock treasure chest number two. These seven keys are the only way you can unlock the most abundant life on earth that God has waiting just for you.

⌐—⊙ The First Key: Become a Christian

Great news! You already have a big head start! You already know what the first key is! The first key to having an abundant life on Earth is to become a Christian. The first three chapters just addressed that in detail. Hopefully, you have already found this key. It is impossible for a person who has never truly become a Christian to have the most abundant life possible here on Earth. Many people try in vain to do so. Most of the estimated one hundred thousand–plus people who die and enter Hell each and every day are probably trying (unsuccessfully) to craft the best life they can by their own efforts. If you are still not 100 percent certain you will go to Heaven when you die, please humble yourself and sincerely pray the prayer on page 44 of this book. God will richly reward you with eternal life in Heaven as we previously discussed in treasure chest number one. As a bonus, you will have also found the first key to treasure chest number two as well. This is your first step to a truly abundant life on Earth.

Most people in the world waste their entire lives trying to be successful or happy or rich according to the world's ever-twisting standards. True Biblical success, peace and joy are only possible through a proper relationship with God and with healthy, Godly relationships with the people around you. Worldly success usually focuses on selfish and prideful ambitions for wealth, power, and fame. These often lead to greed, materialism, becoming a workaholic, addictions, lust, immorality, dishonesty, unethical business or social activities, vanity, and prioritizing selfish desires above Godly things in our life. Biblical abundant life is much, much better. Once you have tasted the abundant life God has for you, you will realize that worldly success, with which much of the media and the advertising industry tries to brainwash us, is only a cheap, inferior, usually corrupted substitute.

Satan cleverly uses our selfish, materialistic ambitions and our increasingly busy schedules to crowd God out of our lives little by little. So often, people comment or complain about how busy they are. Many people have been fooled into believing that having a very busy life is a sign of success. I am becoming more and more convinced that Satan is directly behind most of our overly busy and hectic schedules. Satan keeps us too busy and tempts our obsessive desires for material success just to distract us from God. Satan appears to be succeeding at this way too much.

God deserves much more than just a token amount of your leftover time and energy at the end of a hectic week. God wants you to put Him first in every part of your life. Unclutter your life. Make more quality time for God. He can make your life less hectic. If you seek God first in every aspect of your life, He will take care of your every need. Jesus Himself warned us to not worry so much about material things, "For the pagans run after all these things, and your Heavenly Father knows that you need them. But seek *first* His kingdom and His righteousness, and all these things will be given to you as well" (Matthew 6:32–33, NIV; emphasis added). In the same chapter, Jesus also said, "No one can serve two masters. Either he will hate the one and love the other, or he will be devoted to the one and despise the other. You cannot serve both God and money" (Matthew 6:24, NIV1984). The Holy Bible is often so simple yet so profound. Don't prioritize money, jobs, careers, homes, cars, or even family first in your life. Don't be a slave in a rat race for temporary material *things*. Simply prioritize God first in all parts of your life. God will help you with the rest of your life much better than you could ever help yourself. One of the great hymns says it well: "Turn your eyes upon Jesus, look full in His wonderful face, and the *things* of earth will grow strangely dim, in the light of His glory and grace."

The greatest things in life are not *things*. Doing something for yourself and for others you love that has eternal value is far greater. For the mere cost of one or two such things in your life you could almost certainly live without, you could lovingly give copies of this book and share God's greatest treasures with everyone in your own personal sphere of influence. God's eternal treasures are infinitely better than temporary things.

As a Christian there is an exciting world waiting for you—even before you get to Heaven! Becoming a Christian is the first key to treasure chest number two. You now have the First of seven keys to your abundant life treasure!

The Second Key: The Holy Bible

The second key to having an abundant life on Earth is to read at least a few pages of the Holy Bible each day. You will feel better, and you will quickly become wiser about God and about those things that are really important in your own life. Your daily focus will be drawn away from the less important, often spiritually distracting and destructive things in the world around us.

Remember, the Holy Bible is God's word, so there is no better source of information or guidance for every aspect of our daily lives. The Holy Bible is like God's owner's manual for our life. Psalm 119:105 says, "Your word is a lamp to my feet and a light for my path" (NIV1984). 2 Timothy 3:16 says, "All scripture is God-breathed and is useful for teaching, rebuking, correcting and training in righteousness, so that the man of God may be thoroughly equipped for every good work" (NIV1984). The Holy Bible is as relevant to us today as when it was written. "For the word of God is living and active. Sharper than any double-edged sword, it penetrates even to dividing soul and spirit, joints and marrow; it judges the thoughts and attitudes of the heart" (Hebrews 4:12, NIV1984). Jesus said, "Man does not live on bread alone, but on every word that comes from the mouth of God" (Matthew 4:4, NIV1984). The world would be a much better place if we all read and lived by the Bible more than all the other less important things we read. Of course, we need to *apply* what we read in the Bible to our everyday lives. If we read it and ignore it, we have not accomplished much! "Do not merely listen to the word, and so deceive yourselves. Do what it says" (James 1:22, NIV1984).

The Holy Bible beautifully proclaims Jesus Christ as Savior and Lord. It tells us the one and only way we can have our sins forgiven and be eternally reconciled to God. The Holy Bible shows us the only way to Heaven, as the preceding chapters summarized just for you. It also gives us all the secrets to having the best life possible on earth (which this chapter highlights just for you.) God has ensured that the Holy Bible remains, by far, the most trusted, most published, most read, most talked about, most widely distributed book in the most languages the world has ever known. It is by far the greatest book ever written. The Holy Bible contains God's inspired words to us. The wisdom found in God's word can make all of our lives much better. This book proudly exalts and directly quotes over two hundred of the all-time best Bible verses—literally the Holy Bible's greatest hits! It references in context over one thousand more for you to explore later. Just reading and heading the two hundred Bible verses lovingly incorporated here in context is guaranteed to change a person's life like nothing else can!

If you would like to read your Bible more (and we all should since it's the second key to having an abundant life) here are some great ideas God will honor in your life:

📖 Try to read some of the New Testament every day. Most Christian theology is found in the New Testament. Also read from Psalms and

Proverbs every day. You will find all these very applicable to our everyday lives. Read them daily, and you will have a nicer day! ☺

   📖 Keep a Bible handy wherever you go, not just at home. Keep one at work and one in your car. Whenever you have a minute or two to spare, read a few verses or an entire chapter. You'll be amazed how much it helps you throughout your day! Let God's word brighten your day as often as you can. Others will see God's light shining through you. From numerous personal experiences, I guarantee you the Holy Bible on your desk or in your car or briefcase will bear fruit as others pass your way.

   📖 Reading your Bible more makes a great New Year's resolution, but it is much more important than most other New Year's resolutions. Reading your Bible more will improve your life more than almost any other New Year's resolution. Commit yourself to read the Holy Bible every day. Make it part of your daily routine. Your life will improve as a result. But make this life-changing resolution today. Don't wait for New Year's!

   📖 Try to read an entire book of the Bible at one sitting, whenever you can. That way, you get the full message together in context. Some quality study Bibles also have very interesting introductions to each book of the Bible. There are twenty-seven books in the New Testament. So if you read at least one per day, you can easily read the entire New Testament in less than one month. That alone will change your life for the better in many ways. I recommend reading through the entire New Testament from Matthew through Revelation before starting the entire Old Testament.

📖 The book of Revelation is a wild ride, so hold on tight! Revelation gets more interesting every time I read it! The last book of the Holy Bible tells of the coming apocalypse. It is ultimately a book of hope and encouragement for all of God's children. Yet, it will be a terrible time for those who reject God. Revelation is also unique in that God promises special blessings in the first chapter, and again in the last chapter, upon anyone who will read it and heed it. Revelation 1:3 says, "Blessed is the one who reads the words of this prophesy, and blessed are those who hear it and take to heart what is written in it, because the time is near" (NIV1984). At Revelation 22:7, Jesus says, "Behold, I am coming soon! Blessed is he who keeps the words of the prophesy in this book" (NIV1984). While beyond the scope of this book, the Holy Bible's apocalyptic writings are fascinating! They literally eclipse the world's best dramatic thrillers or suspense stories ever written or filmed.

Fascinating End-Time Apocalyptic and Prophetic Bible Passages

If you would like to read more real prophesy about the end times, antichrist, tribulation, the second coming of Jesus, and other very intriguing matters related to the book of Revelation and beyond, the following passages will give you a very strong foundation. To go deeper still, use a quality study Bible and read all the commentaries analyzing each verse.

- Isaiah 2 and 11:10–13 and 65:17–25
- Ezekiel 37–39
- Daniel 7–12
- Joel 1–3
- Zechariah 12 and 14
- Malachi 4
- Matthew 19:28 and 24–25
- Mark 13
- Luke 21
- John 14:1–4 and 14:28–31
- Acts 1:7–11 and 3:19–21
- Romans 1:18–32
- 1 Corinthians 15:22–28 and 15:35–58
- Philippians 3:20–21
- 1 Thessalonians 4:13–5:11 and 5:23–24
- 2 Thessalonians 2
- 1 Timothy 4:1–5
- 2 Timothy 3:1–9
- Titus 2:11–14
- Hebrews 9:22–28 and 10:24–31

- 2 Peter 1:20–21 and 2–3
- 1 John 2:15–3:3
- 2 John 1:7
- Jude 1:1–25
- Revelation 1–22

📖 If you have a red-letter edition of the Bible, the words Jesus personally spoke will be conveniently highlighted for you in red print. His actual words are always very interesting and profound. Most of Jesus's words (in red) appear in the four gospels Matthew, Mark, Luke and John. A few more can be found in the books of Acts and Revelation. Sometimes it is nice to just pick up your Bible and read some of Jesus's actual words. Think of Jesus being right there with you speaking those very words that literally changed the course of human history. The greatest and wisest person to ever live—the Son of God–can speak to you today. Jesus's words alone will change your life for the better. They are really that powerful. With a red-letter edition of the Holy Bible this could not be easier.

📖 If you read the New Testament at least twelve minutes per day, you can read it all in about three months. That would mean reading about three to four chapters per day. Most chapters are only a few pages long. Of course, reading more is better. You can read the entire New Testament in a month by reading at least thirty minutes per day. You can read it in about two weeks by reading about one hour per day. The more you read it, the more you will love it! Deeper and deeper layers of meaning will be revealed to you by God, even when you read some passages countless times.

📖 If you read the entire Holy Bible at least twelve minutes per day, you can read it all in one year. That would mean reading about three to four chapters per day on average. If you read it about half an hour per day, you can finish it in about six months. If you read the Holy Bible at least an hour per day, you can finish it in less than three months. It takes an estimated seventy to eighty hours to read the entire Holy Bible. Some might say an adventure of a lifetime would be to go around the world in eighty days. The Holy Bible will take you—so much more profoundly—around the universe in eighty hours! God has blessed me with extensive travels to twenty five foreign countries and most of the fifty States. Nevertheless, my journeys through the Holy Bible have personally helped me the most. People in every country on Earth need Jesus and the treasures in the Holy Bible more than anything else.

📖 Try to read from a quality study Bible whenever you can. That way when you have a question about something, the commentary right there on the page is often very helpful. Biblical history and archaeology are fascinating, especially as you come to realize this is how God Almighty, the Creator of the universe has chosen to relate to mankind. Two of the most popular study Bibles of all time are the NIV Study Bible (which contains one of the most outstanding assortments of Bible study resources in a single volume) and the Life Application Study Bible NIV. They have excellent commentaries, maps, charts, cross-references, and a very good concordance that make Bible study even more rewarding. Of course, your local Christian book store has a wide selection of Bibles and study Bibles to choose from. Bibles also make great gifts. The best investment of money you will ever make is buying a high quality study Bible, reading it every day, and following its unsurpassed wisdom in your life. You'll find that the more you study it, the more you'll love it. I hope and pray that this book, Three Treasure Chests, serves as a catalyst for many to explore the vast treasures of the Holy Bible much more than ever before.

📖 People sometimes ask about what is the best translation of the Holy Bible to read. I recall a simple yet profound anecdote about the famous evangelist Billy Graham that contains perhaps the best advice about Bible versions. Apparently, Billy Graham was once asked which Bible version is the best. "The one you read," he replied. I agree. To go a step further, select whatever translation of the Bible you will read from the most. My personal research indicates that, for word-for-word translational accuracy, the New American Standard Bible (NASB) is at or very near the top of the list. Also widely recognized for their translational accuracy are as follows: the English Standard Version (ESV), the Holman Christian Standard Bible (HCSB), and the New English Translation (NET). Regardless, most of us would do very well to simply take our own favorite Bible and simply read it and heed it much more. As the author, I seek Biblical accuracy throughout these pages. I sincerely strive for every word and thought here to glorify God and accurately reflect his most profound words in the Holy Bible, changing countless lives, ultimately changing the world.

My heart sank for millions of Americans and the United States as a whole when I read a survey about Bible reading. Gallup News Service reported October 20, 2000, that more than half of all Americans read the Bible less than once a month including 41 percent who say they rarely or never read it. God, please forgive us. Please turn our eyes back on You and Your word. As our nation ignores God and the Holy Bible more and more, our social, moral, legal, ethical, criminal, financial, and political problems correspondingly grow. This is correlation and causation, not merely coincidence. Politicians have some aspirin and Band-Aids. Christians hold the cure. We need to quit selfishly holding the cure and immediately start lovingly, passionately sharing the cure with everyone around us.

Reading and heeding the wisdom in the Holy Bible can and will transform your entire life in countless ways. If everyone in the world would read and heed the Holy Bible, most wars would never start. Most social problems in the world would end or improve tremendously. The Holy Bible has the best solutions for world hunger, homelessness, disease, crime, corruption, and so on. The greatest commandment in the Holy Bible can be summarized best by the phrase, "Love God and love others." If we would each sincerely love God and love each other today, tomorrow would astound us! One way each of us can make the world a better place is to read our Bibles more every day and simply do what it says. Jesus said of the Holy Scriptures, "If anyone loves me, he will obey my teaching. My Father will love Him, and we will come to him and make our home with Him" (John 14:23, NIV 1984).

Let me end this section with three Holy Bible secrets that will very simply, yet very profoundly, transform your life:

Secret number one: Read the Holy Bible every day before you read anything else.

Secret number two: Read the Holy Bible every day before you listen to the radio or watch TV or social media.

Secret number three: Read the Holy Bible every day more than you read anything else.

God's word—with its divine guidance, wisdom, and love—will transform your life as never before.

From the bottom of my heart, helping as many people as possible read and heed the Holy Bible more is what motivates me to write every word here.

Congratulations! You now have the second key to treasure chest number two: regular Bible study. You now have the second key to your abundant life!

⚷The Third Key: Prayer

The third key to having an abundant life on earth is to effectively *pray* to God regularly every day. Prayer is simply talking to God. Talk to God every day when you are by yourself. A healthy prayer life includes several different kinds of prayer we should all practice regularly, including prayers of praise, thanksgiving, confession, intercession, and petition. *Praise* God for how great He is. *Thank* God for the good things He has blessed you with in your life (i.e., family, friends, health, freedom, food, home, the beauties of nature, individual successes, fun times, etc.). When you sin (and we all do), *confess* your sin to God and ask God to forgive you. Then ask anyone you have hurt to forgive you too. Always remember, God knows every sin you ever commit, even if no one else in the world knows about it. God knows our every thought. Ask God to help you turn away from that sin in your life. Pray for other people who are having problems too, not just for yourself. This is called *intercessory* prayer as you are asking God to help others. Similarly, ask or *petition* God to help you with your own problems—big problems and little problems. Even though you may personally have a solution to a problem, God may help you find a better one. Finally, ask God questions about things you do not understand. Prayer allows you access to the awesome, unlimited power, knowledge, and resources of God Almighty, the architect and creator of the universe. Most people, even most Christians, need much *more* prayer in their lives (think quantitatively). Most Christian's prayers could also be much more *effective* (think qualitatively). Here's how:

The Holy Bible clearly teaches us how to pray most *effectively*. The following are some of the most valuable prayer lessons taken directly from the Holy Bible. They can improve almost anyone's prayer life. Your prayers can change your own life. Your prayers can change the lives of those around you. Your prayers can literally change the world if you will just pray as God intended. Sincerely, from the bottom of my heart, helping as many people as possible pray more effectively is what motivates me to write every word here. I faithfully trust God is helping me help you—and many others—change our great nation and the world for the better in many ways through *more* effective prayers.

Realize that prayer is powerful and can accomplish great things. "The prayer of a righteous man is powerful and effective" (James 5:16, NIV1984). A sincere Christian can accomplish more true and lasting good in the world with prayer, than the president and other world leaders can achieve without prayer. Of course, also having the most prayerful, most sincere Christian president possible, along with other sincere Christian elected leaders, is always best. Strong yet humble, faithful, prayerful Christian leaders can help our great country and the world much better with God's loving, compassionate wisdom, guidance, and blessing than without it.

Pray with *faith*. Jesus said, "I tell you the truth, if you have faith as small as a mustard seed, you can say to this mountain, 'Move from here to there' and it will move. Nothing will be impossible for you" (Matthew 17:20, NIV1984). Here, Jesus had just told his followers their prayers were not answered because they had so little *faith*.

Pray often. Most people simply do not pray enough. Also, don't just pray selfish prayers. James 4:2–3 says, "You do not have, because you do not ask God. When you ask, you do not receive, because you ask with wrong motives, that you may spend what you get on your pleasures" (NIV1984). Pray more selfless prayers such as praising God for His vast greatness and thanking God for His many blessings. This will bring a healthier balance to your prayer life making your other prayers more effective.

Here is a prayer Jesus modeled for us. Many call it the Lord's Prayer. Jesus said,

"And when you pray, do not be like the hypocrites, for they love to pray standing in the synagogues and on the street corners to be seen by men. I tell you the truth, they have received their reward in full. But when you pray, go into your room, close the door and pray to your Father, Who is unseen. Then your Father, Who sees what is done in secret, will reward you. And when you pray, do not keep on babbling like pagans, for they think they will be heard because of their many words. Do not be like them, for your Father knows what you need before you ask Him.

"This, then, is how you should pray:

"Our Father in Heaven, hallowed be Your name, Your kingdom come, Your will be done on Earth as it is in Heaven. Give us today our daily bread. Forgive us our debts, as we also have forgiven our debtors. And lead us not into temptation, but deliver us from evil, for Yours is the Kingdom and the power and the glory forever. Amen."

Matthew 6:5–15 (NIV1984)

Consider incorporating the Lord's Prayer into your daily prayers since Jesus specifically said this was how we should pray. Just try sincerely and thoughtfully praying this along with your other prayers at the very beginning of each day. I faithfully trust God will bless you.

- Prayer brings us closer to God. "The Lord our God is near us whenever we pray to Him" (Deuteronomy 4:7, NIV1984).
- Be *humble* when you pray because "everyone who exalts himself will be humbled, and he who humbles himself will be exalted" (Luke 18:14, NIV1984). Jesus gave a wonderful example of

how prayers of the humble are very effective and how prayers of prideful, self-righteous hypocrites are not. To some who were confident of their own righteousness and looked down on everybody else, Jesus told this parable:

Two men went up to the temple to pray, one a Pharisee and the other a tax collector. The Pharisee stood up and prayed about himself: "God, I thank You that I am not like other men – robbers, evildoers, adulterers – or even like this tax collector. I fast twice a week and give a tenth of all I get.' But the tax collector stood at a distance. He would not even look up to Heaven, but beat his breast and said, 'God, have mercy on me, a sinner.' I tell you that this man, rather than the other, went home justified before God. For everyone who exalts himself will be humbled, and he who humbles himself will be exalted.

Luke 18:9–14 (NIV1984)

Humility and prayer can heal nations too. God said, "If My people, who are called by My name, will humble themselves and pray and seek My face and turn from their wicked ways, then will I hear from Heaven and will forgive their sin and will heal their land" (2 Chronicles 7:14, NIV1984). If Christians will faithfully do exactly what this verse says, our great nation and the world will be healed far beyond what any politicians might achieve alone. Christians can lovingly and peacefully change the world with Godly wisdom and compassion through humble prayer, repentance, and obedience as we help others in need.

- Use prayer in every aspect of your life. "Pray in the Spirit on all occasions with all kinds of prayers and requests" (Ephesians 6:18, NIV1984).

- Make prayer a priority in your life. "Devote yourselves to prayer" (Colossians 4:2, NIV1984).

- Pray a lot more. "Be joyful always; pray continually; give thanks in all circumstances, for this is God's will for you in Christ Jesus" (1 Thessalonians 5:16–18, NIV1984).

- Devote appropriate times and places to prayer. "Very early in the morning, while it was still dark, Jesus got up, left the house and went off to a solitary place, where He prayed" (Mark 1:35, NIV1984).

- Pray for everyone, even your enemies. Jesus said, "But I tell you: Love your enemies and pray for those who persecute you, that you may be sons of your Father in Heaven. He causes His sun to rise on the evil and the good, and sends rain on the righteous and the unrighteous" (Matthew 5:44–45, NIV1984). Jesus, at His crucifixion, and even Stephen at his stoning both prayed for God to forgive their very *executioners*. (See Luke 23:34 and Acts 7:59–60, respectively.) As hard as it may seem, pray for your enemies.

- Seek God's will, not just our own wishes. We should always want God's will to be done in our lives. Just before His crucifixion, Jesus prayed to

God, "My Father, if it be possible, may this cup be taken from Me. Yet not as I will, but as You will" (Matthew 26:39, NIV1984).

 Prayer can cure anxiety and stress. "Do not be anxious about anything, but in everything, by prayer and petition, with thanksgiving, present your requests to God" (Philippians 4:6, NIV1984).

 Prayer and *fasting* together are sometimes necessary for prayers to be answered. "So we fasted and petitioned our God about this, and He answered our prayer" (Ezra 8:23, NIV1984). Jesus said that some things can only be achieved "by prayer and fasting" (Mark 9:29, NIV1984). Some in Jesus's day would fast "twice a week" (Luke 18:12, NIV1984). Fasting is not fashionable in our modern society choked with endless multimillion-dollar food advertisements and restaurants on every corner. But fasting is Biblical. Our generation's neglect of fasting with prayer probably accounts for many unanswered prayers and, as a result, a correspondingly large portion of the moral decline of modern society. Many heroes of faith in the Holy Bible fasted, including Jesus, Paul, Moses, David, Elijah, Esther, and Anna. So did many great Christian leaders since Biblical times, including Martin Luther, John Calvin, John Knox, John Wesley, and Billy Graham. Of course, Biblical fasting should be done primarily for spiritual reasons. Any physical benefits that also result (such as weight loss or fitness) may be welcome and healthy, but they should remain secondary to our deeper spiritual goals. For an excellent, detailed discussion of Biblical fasting, I highly recommend the chapter on fasting in the wonderful Christian book entitled, *Celebration of Discipline* by Richard Foster. If Christians would humbly fast more, their prayers would become more effective.

One of the most famous and beautiful prayers in the Bible is the Twenty-third Psalm. Many Christians love it so much they have committed both it and the Lord's Prayer (quoted just above) to memory. They are both great ways to begin our prayers each new day.

The Lord is my shepherd, I shall not be in want. He makes me lie down in green pastures, He leads me beside quiet waters, He restores my soul. He guides me in paths of righteousness for His name's sake. Even though I walk through the valley of the shadow of death, I will fear no evil, for You are with me; Your rod and Your staff, they comfort me. You prepare a table before me in the presence of my enemies. You anoint my head with oil; my cup overflows. Surely goodness and love will follow me all the days of my life, and I will dwell in the house of the Lord forever.

Psalm 23 (NIV1984)

Be sensitive to God answering your prayers. Sometimes he answers prayers in ways you would have never expected. Be patient. God is never late. Sometimes God's answer to your prayer may be for you to wait. Sometimes God's answer is simply no. Sometimes God's "no" today is really a "yes" for a higher purpose at a later time. Sometimes God will let us personally know the reasons for His answers to prayer. Sometimes He won't. Remember, He's God, and we are not. He is the potter; we are the clay. (See Isaiah 64:8.) God knows what is best for us better than we do ourselves. Always have faith that God is in control, even when you don't understand something. Finally, don't forget to thank God for answering your prayers. Some people find keeping a written prayer journal helps them pray more effectively. It can also help you see how faithfully God answers our prayers when we pray effectively, as we should. As it increases our faith, our future prayers are empowered even more.

Sometimes God will answer your prayers through guidance from the Holy Bible itself. Bible study and prayer often work very well together. They both help us to make better decisions in our life every day. They are both very important keys to your treasure chest full of abundant life! So, read your Bible much more. Pray much more. You will never regret it! Through prayer, we speak to God. Through the Holy Bible, God speaks to us. Always expect God's answers to our prayers and His guidance to follow and not contradict the Holy Bible. Faithfully using both prayer and Bible study together synergistically bears much more fruit than either alone.

Praying the way God intended can dynamically transform your life and the world around you. If you want to personally make the world a better place, then pray more and pray more effectively the way God intended. Congratulations! You now have the third key to treasure chest number two: prayer. You are another step closer to unlocking the treasure of abundant life on earth God wants to give you!

⚷ The Fourth Key: Attend Church Regularly

The fourth key to having an abundant life on earth is to attend church regularly. The Holy Bible clearly says, "Let us not give up meeting together" (Hebrews 10:25, NIV1984). Find a church that teaches the Bible accurately and sincerely honors Jesus Christ. Of course, carefully avoid churches related to non-Christian cults or religions previously mentioned in the chapter on Heaven and Hell. Make sure you feel comfortable at your church and attend as often as possible. Even Jesus Himself *regularly* went to a place of worship on the Sabbath day of the week. "On the Sabbath day He went into the synagogue, as was His custom" (Luke 4:16, NIV1984). Each of us should simply follow Jesus's example. Jesus attended church regularly even though He never sinned. So don't kid yourself here. We are all sinners and need to attend church regularly much more than Jesus did. Most excuses for not attending church regularly are really Satan deceiving you in order to harm you somehow. Don't be fooled. If you have truly become a Christian, you should desire to attend church regularly to worship and learn more about God. If you do not truly desire to attend church regularly with other Christians, please honestly ask yourself if you are 100 percent sure you are in fact a Christian. Eternity is way too long to get it wrong! Attending church regularly will improve your life. You will grow into a more mature Christian. Missing church regularly will damage your life and those closest to you. My last pastor used to say that some of the most miserable people he knew were Christians who were out of regular fellowship with their church and with other believers.

Attending church worship, Bible studies, and other activities allows you to spend quality time with other Christians. This will strengthen your character as an individual and as a Christian. It will help you become more knowledgeable about your faith. You will also help others in the same way. Attending church is about much more than what you might personally get out of it yourself. Your regular attendance and participation also affect other people in important ways. Some there need your support. You are also setting an example for those around you, especially your own family, friends, and coworkers. "Let your light shine before men that they may see your good deeds and praise your Father in heaven" (Matthew 5:16, niv1984). As we all mature as Christians, we should think less about how church can help me and more about how I can personally help others through quality church ministries that glorify Jesus. "Let us therefore make every effort to do what leads to peace and to mutual edification" (Romans14:19, niv1984).

I can offer a perfect and potentially far-reaching personal testimonial here. Had I not attended church regularly during the past two decades I would not have been spiritually mentored, when I needed it most, by such godly pastors as Dr. Bob Bender, Dr. Pat Kilby, John Haynes, Bill Leveridge, Jim Gillum, and so many other sincere Christians at the Ada First Baptist Church and Crossway First Baptist Church in Sulphur. *Three Treasure Chests* would not even exist without them. I could never thank them enough, but their treasures in Heaven are bountiful. Countless, precious souls I pray this book touches, God willing, would have suffered had I selfishly chose most any other path short of regular church attendance. Even if we don't see exactly how, rest assured not attending church regularly will significantly hurt you, hurt your family and friends, hurt many others, and dishonor God.

We all must live and work with non-Christians in our society every day. We need to share Jesus's love with them whenever we can. Yet, if you spend too much time around non-Christians you will be influenced negatively. The Holy Bible cautions, "Do not be misled: Bad company corrupts good character" (1 Corinthians 15:33, NIV1984). Christians need to be a positive influence on society, not the other way around. Make it a point to hang around with other Christians whenever you can. Christian friends are wonderful encouragements to each other. "They devoted themselves to the apostles' teaching and to the fellowship, to the breaking of bread and to prayer" (Acts 2:42, NIV1984). Devote yourself to Christian worship, teaching, and fellowship.

Congratulations! You now have the fourth key to treasure chest number two: regular church attendance. You now have the fourth key to *your* abundant life! You only need three more keys to open treasure chest number two!

⌐—◦ The Fifth Key: Tithes and Offerings

The fifth key to having an abundant life on earth is to give tithes and offerings to God in accordance with the Holy Bible. The Holy Bible is very clear that each Christian should regularly give traditionally 10 percent of their earnings as tithes to God. This should normally go to the local church where you regularly attend. All other giving to church ministries, other Christian organizations or many secular charities is fine, but should be prioritized after perhaps 10 percent has been *cheerfully* given to God as a tithe. As Christians, we need to humble ourselves and realize that 100 percent of everything good we have is a blessing from God. God gave us our life and our health and our minds. He gave us our abilities and our opportunities to earn a living, especially in America and other free societies. 100 percent of our income is a blessing from God. James 1:17 says, "Every good and perfect gift is from above, coming down from the Father" (NIV1984). The 10 percent tithe we give back to God acknowledges and shows our sincere appreciation for the 100 percent that God has blessed us with in the first place. Not tithing to

God is akin to not even sincerely thanking a loved one for an expensive gift they give you.

We also tithe because we love God and we love others who will benefit spiritually and physically from our support of quality Christian ministries. Of course, we personally benefit from our own church's ministries as well. We should gladly support them. Have faith that with God's divine guidance and wisdom you can actually live a much better life faithfully on the remaining 90 percent with God's blessing than less faithfully on the 100 percent without God's blessing. God knows your thoughts and motives. "God loves a cheerful giver" (2 Corinthians 9:7, NIV1984).

Beware. If a Christian selfishly refuses to give proper tithes, God views it very seriously as stealing from God. Those who don't attend church regularly, just addressed above, often don't tithe either and fall under God's same curse. God said,

> "Will a man rob God? Yet you rob Me.
> "But you ask, 'How do we rob You?'
> [God replies] "In tithes and offerings. You are under a curse—the whole nation of you—because you are robbing Me. Bring the whole tithe into the storehouse, that there may be food in My house. Test Me in this," says the Lord Almighty, "and see if I will not throw open the floodgates of Heaven and pour out so much blessing that you will not have room enough for it."
>
> Malachi 3:8–10 (NIV1984)

Individuals, as well as America and the other nations generally, could all benefit greatly from heeding God's word in Malachi more. God can and will do more good in our nation and world with Christians' 10 percent faithful tithes lovingly invested in God's ministries than governments will ever do with 20, 30, or 40-plus percent in forced taxes, all too often wasted or mismanaged. Christians could also drastically help America by heeding God's word, "If My people, who are called by My name, will humble themselves and pray and seek My face and turn from their wicked ways, then will I hear from Heaven and will forgive their sin and will heal their land" (2 Chronicles 7:14, NIV1984). The greatest prescription and cure for all that is ailing America, the land that I love, is for Americans, and especially all Christians, to take heed of the two Bible passages just quoted in Malachi and 2 Chronicles and call me in the morning.

Beyond our financial tithing, Christians should also generously and joyfully give of their time and talents to quality Christian ministries as well. What would happen if every Christian gave at least 10 percent of their time to serving God and helping needy people in some way? That alone would drastically change our world. Christians could lovingly remedy most social problems in compassionate, Godly ways far better than many inefficient government programs. Find a way to help in God's work that you enjoy. There is an almost endless array of wonderful Christian ministries in your local church and elsewhere that would love to have your help. Don't be surprised if you are ultimately blessed as much or more than those you are helping.

Jesus commands Christians to be the "salt of the earth" and the "light of the world." (See Matthew 5:13–16.) The roughly one billion Christians worldwide could and should transform the idea of one thousand points of light into literally a "billion points of light" helping those in need all around the globe while reflecting Godly love. If they would each selflessly give just 10 percent of their time, talents, and tithe, Christians could heal our planet like never before. These billion points of light would be not only the light of the world, but the brightest spotlight the world has ever seen. As they lovingly healed our land they would spectacularly shine the spotlight on Jesus and bring praise to God in Heaven.

By the way, we should never tire of helping strangers. "Keep on loving each other as brothers. Do not forget to entertain strangers, for by so doing some people have entertained angels without knowing it" (Hebrews 13:1–2, niv1984).

Congratulations! You now have the fifth key to treasure chest number two: tithes and offerings. You now have the fifth key to your abundant life! Only two more keys to go!

⌐—◦The Sixth Key: Baptism

The sixth key to having an abundant life is to be baptized in accordance with the Holy Bible. Remember, as we saw in the chapter about Heaven and Hell, baptism itself does not save a person. However, every person should be baptized after they become a Christian. When Jesus was being baptized in the Jordan River He set a great example for us. He said, "Let it be so now; it is proper for us to do this to fulfill all righteousness" (Matthew 3:15, niv1984). We should follow the example Jesus set for us, as have millions of Christians over the past two thousand years. Acts 2:41 goes on to say, "Those who accepted His message were baptized" (niv1984). Once you sincerely repent of your sins and faithfully accept Jesus as your Savior and Lord, you *should* be baptized to be obedient to Jesus.

Baptism is a beautiful, symbolic representation of your personal forgiveness and salvation. It will be one of the highlights of your entire Christian life. When you are baptized, you are publicly proclaiming to the world that you have personally repented of your sins and faithfully received Jesus Christ as your Lord and Savior. If you have never been baptized, simply talk to the pastor of your local church. They will be honored and excited to help you. Invite all your family and friends to witness your baptism. It will be very meaningful and a blessing to both you and them. One, or more, of your friends and family might attend your baptism who have not otherwise entered a church in years. Your baptism, faithfully and obediently following Jesus's example, might even help lead them and others to Jesus too!

My three-year-old daughter, Mikayla, likes to dip her fingers into the beautiful baptism pool and waterfall located in our church's atrium. She often says, "When

Jesus comes into my heart, then I can go swimming in there!" A child of only three has touched my heart, and other's hearts who have heard this, with her sweet thoughts of baptism. Be assured, baptism will bless you and those around you.

Update: Since this book was first published in 2013, my daughter, Mikayla, has been saved and then baptized in that very baptismal pool. Further, she has personally witnessed to many of her own friends and watched several of them be baptized there as well. I write this update literally with tears of joy in my eyes for my precious, faithful daughter. Praise God! This is the abundant life!

Well, you now have the sixth key to treasure chest number two: baptism. You are very close to having everything you need for your most abundant life possible on Earth! Treasure chest number two is almost yours!

⚊⊸The Seventh Key: Tell Others about Jesus

The seventh and final key you need to truly have the most abundant life on Earth is so critical, we must devote the entire next chapter to it. You will find your seventh key inside your third and final treasure chest!

Finding and Unlocking
Treasure Chest Number Three:

God's Great Commission

The Great Commission

God commands every single Christian to regularly share the Gospel of Jesus Christ with others. He expects us to personally lead *many* to Jesus throughout our lives and also teach them how to live according to the Holy Bible. This is called the Great Commission. God's word clearly tells us this is *not* just the job of the preacher and church staff, but the vital responsibility of all Christians. Nevertheless, Satan still deceives many otherwise.

In May 1989, the president of the United States *commissioned* me as a United States military officer. Similarly, but more importantly, God commissioned you, me and every other Christian to regularly and effectively share the Gospel of Jesus Christ with all those around us. This is God's Great Commission.

Yet statistically, 98–99 percent of all people worldwide never personally lead even *one* person to saving faith in Jesus during their *entire* life. Most disturbing is that 95 percent of *Christians* today never lead even one person to Jesus in all their life. Let's change that today.

This tragedy of epic proportions has left devastation to millions of lives, families, and eternal souls. No less serious are the dire consequences our broader society as a whole, our nation, and even our world suffers. God is withholding countless blessings from us individually and corporately because of this massive, ongoing, disobedient, rebellious sin for which virtually all of us are accountable. More ominous than missed blessings is that we are greatly provoking God's wrath here. Recall the Holocaust, not many decades ago, where evil, ungodly men unspeakably took six million Earthly lives over the course of four deadly years. Most of us like to think we bear little personal responsibility for that horrible genocide. Yet recall from our brief overview of Hell how at least one hundred thousand lost souls are tragically doomed there each day. Shockingly, that means every *sixty* days over six million lost souls enter Hell forever! This is akin to an eternal spiritual holocaust every two months. It took Hitler years to reach six million, even with Satan's evil unleashed. God's wrath is wholly justified for literally millions of such precious souls whom Christians could and should be reaching much more effectively each and every day.

Every Christian can change this today! You hold the tool in your hands this divine moment in time.

Knowing this, how can Christians even sleep at night until they begin urgently sharing Jesus with others around them? Have we simply let Satan distract us from these things with all the clutter in our lives? Do we even love and care about others enough to do our small part as God has commanded us to do? Satan may be telling you it's someone else's problem, or to just do it later. God's Great Commission in the Holy Bible clearly tells us the exact opposite: It's every single Christian's responsibility to effectively tell others about Jesus now—not later. The excuses God gets every day from 95 percent of us probably only increase God's wrath even more as multitudes unnecessarily and tragically miss Heaven forever.

It is extremely significant the Great Commission served as Jesus's final words for us to follow. In the Holy Bible, all four gospels (Matthew, Mark, Luke, and John) plus the book of Acts *repeatedly* command us to effectively share the great news of the Gospel with others, especially our own family and friends. Apparently, 95 percent of us are not doing so as effectively as God commands. When God repeats himself like this, in every gospel and beyond, we had better pay closer attention. We seriously sin—directly disobey God—when we don't.

Early in Matthew, Jesus says, "Come follow me and I will make you fishers of men" (Matthew 4:19, niv1984). Then, Jesus's final words to us in Matthew command us to, "Therefore, go and make disciples of all nations, baptizing them in the name of the Father and of the Son and of the Holy Spirit, and teaching them to obey everything I have commanded you. And surely I am with you always, to the very end of the age" (Matthew 28:19–20, niv1984). Mark records Jesus commissioning us to "go into all the world and preach the good news to all creation" (Mark 16:15, NIV1984). In Luke, Jesus says, "Repentance and forgiveness of sins will be preached in His name to all nations" (Luke 24:47, NIV1984). In John, Jesus tells us to proclaim the good news like he did, "As the Father has sent me, I am sending you" (John 20:21, NIV1984). In the book of Acts, Jesus tells us to witness to others both near and far, "And you will be My witnesses in Jerusalem, and in all Judea and Samaria, and to the ends of the earth" (Acts 1:8, NIV1984). Jesus repeatedly commands every single Christian, not just preachers, to do this. Please realize, common sense dictates that many people are often more receptive to a trusted family member or friend lovingly sharing Jesus with them than even the most well-meaning church staff member they might barely know. Even if you have never witnessed to another person about Jesus in your entire life, you can do so very accurately and effectively today by simply giving them a copy of this book. It could not be easier.

How Many of These Books Should I Give Away?

Now, you might ask yourself: "*Who* should I give copies to and *how many* copies should I share with others?" While there are no magic numbers, I can offer you some logical and helpful Biblical guidance here. Recall for a moment from John 14:2–3 (KJV) that Jesus is preparing mansions in Heaven for all Christians. If you could give numerous brand-new Earthly mansions away to all your closest family and friends, who would you give them to? If the mansions were entirely paid for by someone else, how many would you give away? Many, to be sure! So faithfully trust that God will bless you, and many others, abundantly if you lovingly give a copy of this book to *exactly* the same individuals you would give a free mansion if you could. Any of them who unlock these treasures will truly receive blessings in this life and in the eternal life to come worth far more than an Earthly mansion. Realize, no one in Heaven would ever trade even one day there for the finest Earthly mansion. Simply give a book to whomever you would give a mansion. Personal evangelism could not be simpler. Changing the world could not be easier. Just open up your heart and let God's love flow through you to others.

Similarly ask yourself, how many people do you know that you would love enough to wake them up in the middle of the night and warn them if a huge wildfire were approaching their house? Simple common sense suggests you should immediately tell these exact same people about Hell as lovingly and accurately as possible. If you really care about them, just give them a copy. This book effectively warns others about Hell in a loving and appropriate manner with the right level of urgency. Be a thorn in Satan's side every time you share *Three Treasure Chests* with others. Hell is full enough already.

Interestingly, Jesus saw fit to specifically mention the numbers thirty, sixty and one hundred regarding this very subject in one of His most famous parables, the parable of the Sower. Jesus is specifically talking about sharing God's treasures with others here. Jesus told this parable to large crowds of people, much like you and me. Jesus Himself mentions thirty, sixty, and one hundred twice in Matthew's account and twice as well in Mark's gospel. Luke's account of this parable mentions only the number one hundred. Remarkably, that is five times God saw fit to quote these same numbers in the Holy Bible. God wants each of us to ingrain these numbers in our minds for a very good reason.

So as you read this parable, prayerfully ask yourself if God would be glorified for you to faithfully and lovingly share this book with thirty or sixty or one hundred others: God's numbers, not mine. To begin with, most of us probably have thirty, sixty, or one hundred or more family members and friends we sincerely love or care about. Each of us would go out of our way to offer that many, or more, of our loved ones free mansions if we could. Similarly, each of us would immediately warn that many, or more, of our loved ones of an approaching wildfire if we could. So simultaneously offer them Heavenly mansions and warn them of Hell as soon as you can. Prayerfully read this parable and faithfully go wherever God leads you. You will never regret it. Jesus said,

> A farmer went out to sow his seed. As he was scattering the seed, some fell along the path, and the birds came and ate it up. Some fell on rocky places, where it did not have much soil. It sprang up quickly, because the soil was shallow. But when the sun came up, the plants were scorched, and they withered because they had no root. Other seed fell among thorns, which

grew up and choked the plants. Still other seed fell on good soil, where it produced a crop—a hundred, sixty or thirty times what was sown. He who has ears, let him hear.

Matthew 13:3–9 (NIV1984)

Jesus seldom interpreted his parables, but here He does. Jesus explained the parable of the Sower to His disciples. Jesus continued,

Listen then to what the parable of the sower means: When anyone hears the message about the Kingdom and does not understand it, the evil one comes and snatches away what was sown in his heart. This is the seed sown along the path. The one who received the seed that fell on rocky places is the man who hears the word and at once receives it with joy. But since he has no root, he lasts only a short time. When trouble or persecution comes because of the word, he quickly falls away. The one who received the seed that fell among the thorns is the man who hears the word, but the worries of this life and the deceitfulness of wealth choke it, making it unfruitful. But the one who received the seed that fell on good soil is the man who hears the word and understands it. He produces a crop, yielding a hundred, sixty or thirty times what was sown.

Matthew 13:18–23 (NIV1984)

Please prayerfully read this wonderful parable of our Lord and Savior in Mark 4 and Luke 8 as well. God rarely tells us the same exact thing five times. When

He does, we had better take heed. Share God's treasures however He leads you. I pray for you to be the good soil and have a huge harvest as God is glorified.

Faithfully trust God to guide you as to who you should share his greatest treasures with. Trust God to reveal to you how many people within your own personal sphere of influence you should give copies of *Three Treasure Chests*. Whether God leads you to share it with thirty, sixty, or one hundred others as Jesus mentioned in his parable—or some other number—is between you and God.

Similarly, God wants our lives to be *fruitful* for Him. Jesus's parable of the Vine and the Branches (below) tells Christians to produce fruit, *more* fruit, and ultimately *much* fruit for God. For example, perhaps giving a few of your friends a copy of this book will produce *some* fruit for God in their lives and in yours. That's good. Giving thirty to sixty others a copy will almost certainly produce significantly more fruit. That's even better. However, should you give copies to one hundred–plus people; then I trust that God will use both you and them to produce much fruit, even an abundance. That's best. By all means, be as fruitful for God as you possibly can and you will store up vast eternal treasures in Heaven for yourself and many others as well. Jesus said,

> I am the true vine, and My Father is the gardener. He cuts off every branch in Me that bears no fruit, while every branch that does bear fruit He prunes so that it will be even more fruitful. You are already clean because of the word I have spoken to you. Remain in Me, and

I will remain in you. No branch can bear fruit by itself; it must remain in the vine. Neither can you bear fruit unless you remain in Me. I am the vine; you are the branches. If a man remains in Me and I in him, he will bear much fruit; apart from Me you can do nothing. If anyone does not remain in Me, he is like a branch that is thrown away and withers; such branches are picked up, thrown into the fire and burned. If you remain in Me and My words remain in you, ask whatever you wish, and it will be given you. This is to My Father's glory, that you bear much fruit, showing yourselves to be My disciples.

John 15:1–8 (NIV1984)

Bear *much* fruit if at all possible. Whether God leads you that thirty, sixty, or a hundred apples is much fruit is between you and God. Do your best to glorify our Heavenly Father and show yourself to truly be His disciple. Your third treasure chest will overflow with vast additional treasures in Heaven.

Who Should I Give Copies of This Book To?

It is very important for many reasons that you give *both* Christians and non-Christians copies of this book. Please, do not try to judge which of your family or friends are already Christians and which are not. Judging others is God's job, not ours. (See Matthew 7:1; Luke 6:37; Romans 14:4–13; and James 4:11–12.) It is *very important* that copies of this book go to *all* of your loved ones who are already Christians and also to all of your loved ones who are not yet Christians.

Here's why. Of course, anyone who is not yet a Christian needs to be told immediately how to become a Christian as accurately and thoroughly as we can. They need to know how to escape a horrible eternity in Hell and how to choose a fantastic everlasting life in Heaven instead before it's too late. They need to be made aware of numerous things that deceive so many people today into falsely thinking they are bound for Heaven when, really, they are not. They need to know how God has a wonderful abundant life waiting for them here on Earth even before reaching Heaven too. They also need to learn how to share God's greatest treasures with their own family and friends.

Yet it is equally important that any Christians you know receive a copy of this book. Why? Because they are the ones most likely to take the one seed you plant with them and multiply it into dozens or hundreds or thousands of changed lives. I would almost rather you give your first few copies of this book to the most devoted Christians you know rather than non-Christians for that very reason. Still, we can all agree that it is vitally important to do both as soon as possible. Each one of your loved one's eternal souls is important beyond measure to both you and to them. Additionally, this book can Biblically reassure any Christian of their proper relationship with God. Most importantly, a person can determine if their current path and hope of Heaven is based upon God's one true path to heaven, or on a perilous path rapidly leading to a cliff overlooking

Hell. Additionally, many sincere Christians still have a lot to learn about claiming the abundant life God offers each of us here on Earth. Simply give copies to both Christians and non-Christians. It is vital to do both.

First of all, I challenge you to simply give a copy of this book to each of your closest family and friends, regardless of how religious they might appear. If all Christians would simply share God's greatest treasures with their own family and friends like this, the entire world would be evangelized very quickly. This has been God's design all along. Tragically, 95 percent of us are not following God's design. Our world would change overnight. Many social problems would end or be significantly relieved. God would be glorified as never before. May many souls be saved (treasure chest number one)! May many of your loved ones also find a more abundant life on earth (treasure chest number two)! May all of our additional Treasures in Heaven multiply exponentially (treasure chest number three)!

Consider giving copies to all your coworkers, acquaintances, and anyone depressed or needing encouragement. However, be sensitive when giving a copy to anyone who has recently lost a loved one who might not have been a Christian. Soon after their loss, surviving family members might not be ready for such frank talk about Hell.

If you encounter homeless people asking for help, you might consider giving them a copy of this book. Frankly, they may be more likely to read it if you strategically tuck a dollar or two inside a particular page such as the prayer for salvation on page 44.

Do you wonder if the author of this book practices what he preaches? Well, I am certainly a sinner, but by God's grace my sins have been forgiven. I have failed many times in God's eyes, but He still loves me and uses me anyway. For the first thirty years of my life, I had never personally led even one person to Jesus, statistically just like the other 95 percent of Christians. How sad, even though I had been raised in church by loving Christian parents and grandparents and faithfully trusted Jesus at age nine. That, and many other things, dramatically changed for me on Thanksgiving Day 1993.

That day, I tragically witnessed my beloved dad— who was my lifelong hero, business partner, mentor, and best friend—have a horrible car accident that would not ultimately claim his life until after he suffered unspeakably in ICU for six weeks. I literally held my dad's—my hero's—severely broken neck in both hands, supporting it to the best of my ability until the ambulance finally arrived on that frigid Thanksgiving Day that still chills my soul today. Adrenaline was the catalyst heightening my own mind and body as my hero paradoxically described progressing pain and paralysis in his body to his only son. Both of us felt paradigms profoundly shifting for Thanksgiving, life, love, eternity, and even God.

From that moment on, God had my attention like never before regarding vital spiritual and eternal things. My deepest soul searching began. Following this dramatic tragedy, I renewed my dedication to God. I rapidly began maturing as a Christian—like I should have done many years before. I could have let that tragedy sour my life. Instead, I determined to take life's lemons and make lemonade for all around me. I became compelled to make absolutely sure that I and, to the best of my ability, my closest loved ones would be reunited with my beloved dad and grandparents one fine day in Heaven with God.

God's growing influence on me through the Holy Bible and prayer in my life ultimately revealed a profound Biblical truth: God expected *every* Christian—not just me in my situation, not just preachers either—to tell others about His greatest treasures. Every Christian needs to passionately know this. God expects every Christian to share Jesus with others. I sincerely hope this book helps you share Jesus with many others for God's ultimate glory.

That year, I authored essentially two different but related essays that would inspire the earlier incarnations of this book. For more than fifteen years, I faithfully gave away personally signed copies of these essays, often specifically tailoring them to best serve a recipient's personality or situation. Years ago, I lost track after lovingly giving away more than one thousand of these signed essays. Through them, God allowed undeserving me the great privilege to humbly lead many others to Jesus, to renew relationships with God, and to find the keys to eternal life in Heaven and Godly abundant lives on Earth. To God be the glory, not me.

Now, many years later, God led me to transform these formerly very personal essays I lovingly used for my own family and friends into *Three Treasure Chests* for the benefit of many others. I prayerfully and faithfully trust that with God's help, you will use this book as a tool to lovingly share God's greatest treasures with your own family and friends much like I did for many hundreds of my own loved ones.

Yes, at times I have failed God. We all will until we are perfected in Heaven. Yet I did freely, lovingly, faithfully, and compassionately share God's greatest treasures with many hundreds of my own family, friends, co-workers, acquaintances, and many strangers. I did so for many years, long before God ever inspired me to challenge you to do the same today within your own personal sphere of influence. If you faithfully do but a small fraction of my humble example here, together we will change the world—not my way—God's way!

I sincerely hope and pray you personally find and unlock all three treasure chests.

I humbly pray for God to use all of us to change America and our world according to his perfect will.

I pray for God to give you the faith, wisdom, courage, and divinely prepared perfect opportunities to share God's greatest treasures with others every day for the rest of your life. I faithfully pray they will, in turn, unlock all these treasures as well. I pray that many will share with many more, who share with many more on down the line as we lovingly grow God's eternal kingdom. *To God be the glory! Thine is the kingdom and the power and the glory forever! Amen.*

Creative Ways to Give Three Treasure Chests to Others

M ost of us would have a blast giving away keys and deeds to thirty or sixty or even one hundred gorgeous mansions, to all our friends! It would be the most *exciting* thing we ever did in our life! Now, realize that sharing God's treasures is ultimately even better! Have a *blast* giving away copies of this book to others! Think of fun and creative ways to do so! Tell someone, "Hey, I want to give you *Three Treasure Chests* right now for free!" Then, just watch their reaction when you really do! Or tell someone, "My friend just gave me *Three Treasure Chests*, and I want to share some treasure with you right now!" Imagine their surprise! "Would you like some *free* treasures? Just ask me!"

Sharing the greatest treasures in the universe with those you care about can be the most exciting and rewarding thing in your life! Try to have as much fun giving your friends copies of this book as if you were really giving them free mansions instead. I know some people on Earth would rather have the mansion. (But frankly, most of us are running a little low on surplus mansions these days—you know, with the economy and all.) Remember, everyone in Heaven or Hell would tell you the treasures offered inside this book are much more valuable than any Earthly mansion anyway. This is the most important thing a Christian can do. It is the most eternally rewarding thing you can ever do. This will be your life's greatest accomplishment. This is the most loving thing you can do for another person.

Using This Book as a Witnessing Tool

Hopefully, the very book you hold in your hand can reinvigorate God's Great Commission in your life and in that of countless others. Prayerfully, many souls can hear about "The Greatest Story Ever Told," God's love, salvation through faith in Jesus, the free gift of eternal life in Heaven, and how to have a Godly, abundant life on Earth, and about the dramatic extremes of Heaven and Hell. Faithfully share copies of this book, *Three Treasure Chests*, with everyone you can, especially your closest family and friends. Make sure they know about God's greatest treasures before it's eternally too late.

This book is designed to dynamically help these 95 percent of Christians, and perhaps the other 5 percent as well, who simply are not witnessing to others as often or as effectively as God expects. As an analogy, I've always loved fishing. God did not *commission* us to become "fishers of men" and then let 95 percent of us never catch even one fish throughout our entire lifetime! Please, don't let the analogy detract from the seriousness of the problem.

This book is also designed to be a more effective way to tell others about God's Treasures because it is simultaneously more Biblically accurate and thorough than many other overly simplified gospel presentations or leaflets and at the same time more passionate and uncompromising. Most intelligent people will not sincerely trust their entire life and eternal soul to Jesus, or anyone else, given limited or inaccurate information. This book encourages thoughtful, sincere, and genuine eternal professions of faith in Jesus Christ and true repentance, rather than more expedient superficial or emotional statements that are less likely to be truly spiritually fruitful.

This book also Biblically goes well beyond many relatively simplistic gospel presentations, which, for brevity's sake, are fairly limited to salvation itself and mostly ignore important discipleship matters. Understood correctly, God's Great Commission is about making "disciples," a much more comprehensive undertaking than a mere one time conversion. A wealth of vital discipleship resources and recommendations are appropriately provided here for the new Christian well beyond most any other type of gospel presentation. Part of discipleship for a new Christian is immediately learning to accurately, effectively, and passionately witness to others. With the *Three Treasure Chests* book in hand—even a brand-new Christian, perhaps having never opened a Bible themselves—could immediately and very effectively witness to their own family and friends simply by sharing copies of this same book with them even on the same day! Over two hundred of the greatest Bible verses are clearly presented in context. Even a crash course in how to pray effectively, which would benefit many mature Christians, is provided.

Even an atheist or agnostic today could realistically read this book and be effectively helping save souls tomorrow. Certainly, a person may witness to others using this book by itself or along with any other witnessing methods they might already find effective. Of course, it seems sharing this book with others must be light years ahead of whatever methods 95 percent of Christians are currently either using so ineffectively or simply are not using at all, regardless of the underlying reasons.

Seventeen Biblical Reasons to Immediately Share Three Treasure Chests with Others

Just like 95 percent of Christians, I never personally led one person to Jesus for the first thirty years of my life. It took the greatest tragedy of my life before I finally realized that I, just like the other 95 percent of Christians, were so chronically disobedient to God in so many ways. Here are at least seventeen strong Biblical reasons why I needed to start effectively sharing God's greatest treasures with others. They apply to every Christian, not just to preachers. If only a couple of them are true, 95 percent of us would still be compelled to act in God's eyes. As you will see, all seventeen are very true and very profound.

1. *Honor God.* Sharing God's greatest treasures with others honors God and brings glory to Him. It is also one of the greatest ways we can say "thank you" to Jesus for what He did for each of us on the cross.

Frankly, we are simply disobedient to God when we don't regularly do so by some effective means such as this. Such disobedience is sin. It dishonors God. This tool is designed to be a simple and effective means that honors God.

2. *The Great Commission.* Sharing God's treasures does our part to fulfill God's Great Commission to share the gospel of Jesus Christ with those around each of us, especially our own family and friends. Paul set a great example for us by telling others the good news "in the hope that I may somehow arouse my own people to envy and save some of them" (Romans 11:14, NIV1984). Simply give copies of this book to all your family and friends within your own personal sphere of influence. God will bless you immeasurably as He simultaneously blesses those you love most.

3. *Greatest commandment.* Sharing God's treasures is obedient to God's two greatest commandments to love God and love others by sharing God's love with others. If we truly love God and love others as we should, we are compelled to share God's greatest treasures with those around us. Sharing God's greatest treasures with your closest family and friends is, without exception, the most loving thing you will ever do for them. This is the greatest gift you will ever offer your loved ones. God's eternal treasures are worth far more than a temporary Earthly mansion. Remember, the best things in life are not *things.*

4. *Golden rule.* Sharing God's greatest treasures is simply just the right thing to do. Jesus himself gave us what many call the "Golden Rule." He said, "So in everything, do to others what you would have them do to you, for this sums up the Law and the Prophets" (Matthew 7:12, niv1984). I would want my closest family and friends to share all of this wonderful information about God's greatest treasures with me now, not later, if they really loved me and sincerely cared about my life and my eternal soul. Therefore, I should share it with them *immediately* if I truly care about them and love them as I should. Simply treat others as you would like to be treated yourself. In this regard, the Golden Rule is just plain common sense.

5. *Change the world.* Sharing God's treasures is the best way we can each change the world for the better, God's perfect way—not by man's corrupt ways. Sharing God's treasures is the most important thing you will ever do after becoming a Christian yourself. Most people want to do something really meaningful with their life. They just don't know how—until today! This is the greatest mission of our lives! Jesus commanded us to be the "salt of the earth" and "the light of the world." (See Matthew 5:13–20.) This is how we preserve, enhance and illuminate the world with God's true light. The more you share God's treasures, the more you brighten the world. Simply share God's gospel of love as much as possible. Realize, this is the most important and meaningful accomplishment of your entire life.

6. *Heaven.* I want to do everything in my power to help as many of my loved ones as possible make it to Heaven with me for eternity. I want every one of them to know accurately and completely the one and only way to have eternal life in Heaven through repentance and faith in Jesus Christ our Savior and Lord. If any of my loved ones don't make it to Heaven, it won't be because I failed to accurately and passionately tell them how to get there. If today were your last day on earth and you could only have one wish, wouldn't you wish that you and your loved ones could spend eternity in Heaven together? Then tell them exactly how to get to Heaven today, not tomorrow.

7. *Hell.* I want to do everything in my power to help as many of my loved ones as possible avoid a terrible eternity in Hell separated from God and their loved ones. An eternal wildfire is ominously approaching the very homes of your family and friends. Please, warn them today, not tomorrow.

8. *Abundant life on earth.* I want all of my loved ones to have the most abundant life possible on earth, with true peace, love, joy, and hope according to the Holy Bible. I want them all to know how much better it is than Satan's vastly inferior, corrupted, perverted substitutes of selfish greed for money, power and fame, lust, materialism, and things.

9. *Additional treasures in heaven.* I look forward to enjoying many additional treasures in Heaven myself, beyond the blessings I share with others. After you personally become a Christian and

unlock the secrets of a Godly, abundant life on Earth, your greatest achievements will be manifesting additional treasures in Heaven. In the Holy Bible, Jesus tells us,

> Do not store up for yourselves treasures on Earth, where moth and rust destroy, and where thieves break in and steal. But store up for yourselves treasures in Heaven, where moth and rust do not destroy, and where thieves do not break in and steal. For where your treasure is, there your heart will be also.
>
> No one can serve two masters. Either he will hate the one and love the other, or he will be devoted to the one and despise the other. You cannot serve both God and money.
>
> Matthew 6:19–21 and 24 (NIV1984)

So how do you store up for yourself these additional treasures in Heaven that Jesus personally commanded us to do? While anything we do that has true eternal value might translate into treasures in Heaven, one thing eclipses them all. Telling others the good news of Jesus Christ blesses others greatly and rewards you with additional treasures in Heaven. Accurately telling others how to get to Heaven and escape Hell can heroically save and rescue them and simultaneously store up more Heavenly treasure for yourself. Show your loved ones how they can exchange eternal suffering and hopelessness for Heavenly mansions of glory. Help others find the keys to unlock their own abundant life on earth and God will overflow your Heavenly blessings beyond your wildest imaginations. Undoubtedly, one of our many Heavenly treasures will be the very presence of our loved ones there with us, for all eternity, that we sincerely, lovingly, and obediently help get there.

Simply put, every time you share these treasures with others, you personally receive additional priceless treasures yourself. That's the essence of treasure chest number three, additional treasures in Heaven. As we lovingly bless others, God showers us with even greater blessings. We can never out give God.

The instant you share this book with another, you immediately inherit priceless additional treasures in Heaven simply for your obedience to God. You hit a home run when the person you share it with truly finds treasures themselves. You hit a grand slam when those you give it to share it with others on down the line, and so on. For any life you touch like this, either directly or indirectly, even complete strangers far down the line, you continue to inherit vast additional treasures in Heaven. So do any others involved. Praise God! Everything good is from Him—especially all these treasures! Of course, as we mature as Christians our true passion for doing these things transitions to sincere, agape love for God and others, not just a love of treasures. God knows our hearts and motives.

10. *Voices from heaven.* Our loved ones in Heaven would probably tell us to passionately and urgently share God's three greatest treasures with others all

around us if they could speak to us today. Ironically, paradoxically, those in Hell would likely give us the same passionate, urgent advice from the exact opposite perspective. As Jesus's parable of the Rich Man and Lazarus (from Luke 16) taught us, even those in Hell today desperately cry out for us to warn their loved ones before its eternally too late for them too.

11. *More effective prayers.* I want all those around me to have some of the most valuable prayer lessons taken directly from the Holy Bible. The most effective prayers can literally change the world for the better. They can make our individual lives better. The brief, yet profound, entirely Biblical prayer lessons within these pages can help each of our prayer lives be much more effective.

12. *The Holy Bible's greatest hits.* I want to give my closest family and friends a copy of this book so they can read in fascinating context more than two hundred of the most famous and life changing verses from the Holy Bible lovingly woven like a hand-made tapestry into these pages just for you like never before. God promised us that wherever His word goes out, it will accomplish His divine purposes. Over one thousand more dynamic verses are referenced for the reader as well.

As the rain and snow come down from Heaven and do not return to it without watering the earth and making it bud and flourish, so that it yields seed for the sower and bread for the eater, so is My word that goes out from My mouth: It will not return to Me empty, but will accomplish what I desire and achieve the purpose for which I sent it.

Isaiah 55:10–11 (NIV1984)

Simply sharing over two hundred of the greatest Bible verses of all with our own loved ones is, in and of itself, reason enough to do so. I faithfully believe God will accomplish His divine purposes as a result.

13. *Eternal investment.* I want to give each of my closest family and friends a copy of *Three Treasure Chests* because the minimal cost required for each of my loved ones is probably the single best investment anyone will ever make in their life and for their eternal soul. Frankly, more significant everlasting good is likely to come from the few dollars I spend on these books than on 99.9 percent of the dollars I spend on everything else in my life. Even much of what I spend specifically on these books will ultimately be reinvested in printing and distributing more books to bless more people on down the line around the world. I can be a vital part of the single greatest mission on the planet for God's ultimate glory.

14. *Thank you.* Sharing copies of this book is a great way to express your appreciation to someone or simply to say thank you for most any occasion. You could even handwrite a note on the inside cover of this book such as,

May God's Three Greatest Treasures always remind you that I sincerely Treasure your love and friendship. Thank you for your kindness.

*Love,
Mikayla*

15. *Lovingly help strangers.* Beyond my own family and friends, as God leads me, I want to occasionally give copies of *Three Treasure Chests* to other people, perhaps even strangers whenever God leads me to do so. Recall, the Holy Bible says, "Do not forget to entertain strangers, for by so doing some people have entertained angels without knowing it" (Hebrews 13:2, NIV1984). For example, I may feel led to specially bless someone I would normally give tips for their service, such as waiters and waitresses at restaurants, taxi drivers, valets, hotel workers, hairstylists, and so on. It is exciting to imagine how one kind gesture like this might drastically change their lives for the better—perhaps more than anything anyone might ever do for them. It is even more exciting to imagine that my initial spark of generosity might inspire at least some of them to give copies of this book to many, many others on down the line whom I may never even know this side of Heaven. I may be starting a chain reaction changing countless lives I do not yet even know. Making the world a better place is a great reward besides the unlimited Heavenly rewards that may follow. One fine day, it will be so exciting to be in Heaven and have strangers, perhaps many, hugging

me, forever grateful, because of seeds I planted or watered that eventually grew into their eternal salvation! You can truly become that blessed person the profoundly beautiful song "Thank You" by Ray Boltz imagines on that divine day in Heaven.

> One by one they came far as your eyes could see;
> Each life somehow touched by your generosity.
> Little things that you had done, sacrifices you made,
> They were unnoticed on the earth, in Heaven now
> Proclaimed!
> Thank you for giving to the Lord.
> I am a life that was changed.
> Thank you for giving to the Lord.
> I am so glad you gave.

16. *Guide or outline.* Sometimes, after you give someone a copy, just faithfully trust God and his Holy Spirit to do the rest and diligently pray to those ends. Other times, you may also feel led to personally discuss God's love with someone further in addition to simply giving them a copy of this book. Feel free to use this book as a tool or a guide or an outline, so you don't have to remember everything they might ask you about. Try to be sensitive and obedient to however God might lead you in each individual situation. God is infinitely smarter than we are. Faithfully trust that God will help you share His love with others.

17. *A ten-in-one tool.* I want to share God's greatest treasures specifically using this book because it uniquely *equips* me with so many awesome things

to share in such a small package. The *Three Treasure Chests* book equips me with the perfect tool to share God's good news with everyone around me. They say dynamite comes in small packages! The greatest treasures on Earth and in the entire universe are clearly and passionately explained here! In this small book, readable in just a couple of hours, I can offer my loved ones the following very profound treasures:

1. Treasure chest number one: eternal life in Heaven
2. Treasure chest number two: abundant life on Earth
3. Treasure chest number three: additional treasures in Heaven
4. The story of Jesus Christ in "The Greatest Story Ever Told"
5. An accurate Biblical description of Heaven and Hell
6. A Biblically accurate and complete prayer of salvation that can be used by anyone anytime, anywhere
7. Warnings about many commonly misunderstood paths that don't lead to Heaven
8. Biblical lessons to make your prayers more effective
10. Creative ways to share all these treasures with all of your family and friends

This book is designed to be the best tool to easily, effectively, inexpensively, accurately and thoroughly share God's love with everyone you know. Each book you share offers the reader so many of God's greatest treasures.

If you want to be a part of God's greatest enterprise, great! God will bless you in many ways with many treasures! Just give others copies of this book. To do this, you do *not* have to have a religious education or background or education of any kind. You do not have to memorize anything. You do not have to attend an eight-week seminar. You do not have to fill out weeks of home work in a workbook. You do not have to uncomfortably disturb strangers in the evening during their dinner and family time. This is perhaps the least threatening yet most persuasive and thorough way to share God's greatest treasures with others. Simply give others copies of this book anyway you can just because you truly care about them.

We've just seen at least seventeen excellent, entirely Biblical reasons why each person should make it a priority in their life to share God's greatest treasures with others. If only one or two of these seventeen profound reasons are true, we are compelled to do so— with a sense of urgency—to the best of our ability.

Practical Ideas to Get You Started

There are *endless* ways to give these three treasure chests to others. Be *creative* yourself. Have *fun* helping others! Anyway, here are some practical, common sense ideas to get you started.

1. Simply hand a copy of this book to anyone you know. Tell them how much you liked reading it. Tell them you hope they enjoy it too. You might even tell them that you are giving a copy of it to

all your friends or to all your family or to everyone you know and love in a manner to make them feel special. You might even consider personally signing the book from you to make it that much more special to them. Write a special, personal note inside the cover if you like or on a piece of stationery to tuck inside.

2. Give a copy of *Three Treasure Chests* as a gift for any occasion (Christmas, birthdays, Easter, Mother's Day, Father's Day, Grandparents' Day, promotion, Valentine's Day, anniversaries, Weddings, graduations, for New Year's resolutions, a new job, secret pals, and so on.) Further, anyone who already looks up to you for any reason would be especially receptive to such a kind gesture—especially from you.

3. Give a copy of this book to your waiter or waitress along with a generous tip. That will be the greatest tip your server ever receives! You just gave them three awesome treasure chests! At the same time, you have just added to your own treasures in Heaven! Who knows, that stranger might greatly multiply that one seed you lovingly and faithfully planted with them.

4. Leave a copy somewhere for someone with a short personal note or letter from you.

5. Leave a copy for someone with an anonymous note or no note at all. Maybe the mystery will add to their intrigue! Mysterious treasures—how perplexing!

6. Mail a copy to someone from you.

7. Mail a copy to someone anonymously.

8. Leave a copy on anyone's doorstep, on their desk, in their office, in their mailbox, at their home, or in their car (either from you personally or anonymously.)

9. Whenever you give someone another gift, slip this book inside the package too—kind of like the surprise in a box of Cracker Jacks! Hopefully, they will find God's treasures far better than a tiny temporary tattoo!

10. Anytime you have an occasion to thank someone for something, give them a copy of this book as an added expression of your appreciation. Perhaps write a personal thank-you note inside the cover as well. This may be the greatest "thank you" of all! It will certainly be the most treasured!

11. If you ever feel like you should personally talk to someone about God, use this book as a tool or an outline. Then you can leave it with them for them to read and think about and pray about after you have gone. They will remember your conversation with them every time they see the book. This would also be a good occasion for you to personally sign the book yourself. They will cherish your love for them, reflecting God's love, every time they read the book or see your signature.

12. Consider making a list (perhaps thirty or sixty or a hundred names long, as God seems to like those numbers in this context) of every family member and friend you would give a free earthly mansion if you could. We've provided you a handy list to use in Appendix A at page 129. Give them the one true path to their own personal Heavenly mansion

instead. Simply mark their names off the list as you give each of them a book leading them to their own mansion in Heaven. One day we will all realize that God's eternal treasures are far better than Earthly mansions anyway.

13. Share this book with all the members of your Bible study group or your Sunday-school class or other church members. Hopefully, they too will each want to give copies to thirty, sixty, or one hundred others themselves! Then the few seeds you initially plant with them may very well grow into a lush garden or a forest! Your treasures in Heaven will grow exponentially as well! You will directly and indirectly bless many others.

14. Share *Three Treasure Chests* with your pastor or other church staff members. Perhaps even direct them to this specific paragraph. They may want to use it as a new tool to equip their church members to easily and effectively spread the good news of Jesus to their community and beyond. This could change your town and beyond if it is God's will. One of the Biblical responsibilities of a pastor and church staff is to equip their church members to spread the good news of Jesus Christ first to their local community and, ultimately, to the world in general. Several places in the Holy Bible speak of *equipping* all Christians to do God's work. This book is specially designed to do exactly that. As mentioned earlier, Ephesians 4:12 says that church leaders are to provide "For the equipping *of* the saints for the work of service, to the building up of the body of

Christ" (NASB and NIV1984). In 2 Timothy 3:17, it says, "So that the man of God may be thoroughly equipped for every good work" (NIV1984). Hebrews 13:20–21 says, "May the God of peace…equip *you* with everything good for doing His will, and may He work in us what is pleasing to Him, through Jesus Christ, to Whom be glory for ever and ever. Amen" (NIV1984). This book is specially designed to be the best tool of its kind to equip Christians to easily, accurately, thoroughly, and effectively share God's love and His awesome treasures with others. The Holy Bible commands *all* Christians, not just preachers and church staff members, to effectively spread the good news of Jesus Christ.

This book can help church leaders equip their members to spread the gospel and grow Godly disciples. To paraphrase Jesus, we should all become "fishers of men." This book doesn't just give others spiritual fish, but it goes much further, in that it teaches and equips them with the right fishing tackle and bait to become spiritual fishermen as God intended. Both the Gospels of Matthew and Mark quote Jesus Christ as saying, "Come, follow Me, and I will make you fishers of men" (Matthew 4:19 and Mark 1:17, NIV1984).

For example, a Sunday-school teacher or pastor could teach a lesson or sermon and give copies of the *Three Treasure Chests* book to some or even all of their class or congregation or members to read in the coming week. Then the following week they could meet again, perhaps with a follow-up lesson or sermon to discuss how best to spark a personal evangelism wildfire for Jesus from that day forward. Certainly, recipients in your community would be attracted to a church who lovingly and freely shared this book with them in the first place. Perhaps include an attractive note or kind letter inviting the recipient to your church. This should spur church growth in a perfectly Biblical manner. This can almost immediately get many more Christians personally involved in the Great Commission like never before. In some communities, increased witnessing, attendance, tithes and offerings may approach or even surpass the cost of books shared by a church with the local community. Don't be surprised if it more than pays for itself financially, let alone spiritually. God is good all the time!

15. This is so easy, even a child can do it. Consider purchasing some reasonable quantities of these books to give to your children, grandchildren, nieces, nephews, or other younger ones, for them to give away to others with your guidance, support, and encouragement. If we simply teach children to effectively share God's treasures when they are young, as we all should be doing, then they will likely continue to do so throughout their adult lives. "Train a child in the way he should go, and when he is old he will not turn from it" (Proverbs 22:6, NIV1984). Imagine the countless additional treasures in Heaven for both you and the child you teach throughout both of your lives. If a child scribbles their name inside the cover, perhaps even

in crayon or magic marker, and hands it to a loved one, perhaps with a sweet hug or kiss, I'll bet that loving grandparent, aunt, uncle, cousin or friend might read it just a little more closely. That innocent child's loving, personal touch might just help save someone's eternal soul. That young child might very well do what 95 percent of adults have not.

16. Never worry that someone might accidentally be given more than one book from different friends. That is really a nice *problem* to have, because then they will already have a few extra copies to pass on down the line to others in their own respective sphere of influence! This "problem" sounds more like an *abundance* to me! Let's see this glass as half full.

17. Try to keep a few of these small books handy and easy to get to wherever you go. For example, keep one or two in your pocket or purse just for that unexpected opportunity we all have experienced when we wish we had a very special little something to give someone. Keep a few copies in your car, at work, at home, and when you travel. I will faithfully guarantee you rewarding opportunities will come your way. Think of them as divine appointments from God! Both you and the recipient will be blessed. God will be glorified. Some of those fleeting moments will be forever proclaimed and celebrated in Heaven!

18. Have a treasure chest party! Give all your guests some treasure and maybe some pizza too! Remember, the gospel of Jesus Christ is the "good news." In fact, it's the *greatest* news ever, and everyone needs it

more than anything else. Why not celebrate it! We certainly celebrate many less important occasions.

19. Put this at the very top of your personal bucket list of things you want to do in your lifetime. If you share God's greatest treasures with at least thirty, sixty, or one hundred of your family and friends, the remainder of your bucket list will be so much more meaningful to you and to others. Maybe even combine the two. The day you finally go skydiving, give a copy to your skydiving instructor. (You might want to do that *before* the jump!)

20. Whenever you think of additional fun and/or creative ways to share *Three Treasure Chests* with others, please let us know. Let others know your ideas. We will try to appropriately update our website or possibly even use your best ideas in future editions and printings of this book. Let's spread the word about the best ways to spread the Word!

Now, let's have a little fun with numbers for a moment! Did you realize that if you give a copy of this book to just a dozen people this week and they all do the same next week, and so on, in just ten weeks, that would be more than enough for every person on earth to have one! How exciting! Anyway, you just do your part and trust God to do the rest. God will bless you and those you share this with accordingly. Please pray that we can faithfully print and distribute these books in accordance with God's will and honor Him greatly at all times. We hope and pray that you and your loved ones will make us struggle to keep up with demand!

The great hymn says it so well: "To God Be the Glory!"

> To God be the glory, great things He hath done!
> So loved He the world that He gave us his Son,
> Who yielded His life an atonement for sin,
> and opened the lifegate that all may go in.
> Praise the Lord, praise the Lord, let the Earth hear His voice!
> Praise the Lord, praise the Lord, let the people rejoice!
> O come to the Father thru Jesus the Son,
> and give Him the glory, great things He hath done!

Epilogue

I sincerely hope and pray you have personally received God's awesome gift of eternal life in Heaven. It is the greatest treasure in the universe. It is the single most important thing in your entire life. Behold, your *first* treasure chest!

I similarly hope and pray you have found all seven keys and have personally unlocked God's wonderful gift of an *abundant* life here on Earth. It is the greatest treasure on Earth. It is the second most important thing in your entire life. Behold, your *second* treasure chest!

Ultimately, I sincerely hope and pray you will share God's magnificent treasures with all of your family and friends. I hope you discover how this book equips you with the perfect tool to easily, accurately and thoroughly share God's greatest treasures with everyone you know. Give *Three Treasure Chests* to thirty or sixty or one hundred plus of your own family and friends. It will be the most loving thing you will ever do for them. You will be blessed as you bless your loved ones beyond measure. Hopefully, they will follow your example on down the line. It will be among your greatest accomplishments in your entire life. You will enjoy vast additional treasures in Heaven. Behold, your *third* treasure chest! "Whatever you do, work at it with all your heart, as working for the Lord, not for men, since you know that you will receive an inheritance from the Lord as a reward. It is the Lord Christ you are serving" (Colossians 3:23–24, NIV1984). Beyond being a part of God's great enterprise of saving souls, you will be patriotically and spiritually helping transform America and ultimately changing the world into a better place one priceless soul at a time. For centuries, philosophers have searched for the "meaning of life." You essentially hold it in your hand right now. The meaning of life is to be reconciled with God and have eternal life in Heaven. The meaning of life is to have the abundant life on Earth God has for you. The meaning of life is to share God's greatest blessings with all of your family and friends. Faithfully serving and glorifying God is the meaning of life. Finding God's three greatest treasure chests is the meaning of life. You have found the true meaning of life—far superior to the philosophy of Plato, Socrates, or anyone else. More importantly, one fine day, God Almighty, the Creator of the universe, will welcome you into Heaven and say, "Well done, good and faithful servant! You have been faithful with a few things; I will put you in charge of many things. Come and share your Master's happiness" (Matthew 25:21, NIV1984)!

May God bless you, your family, and friends with all of His greatest treasures!

May God, our Heavenly Father, and Jesus Christ, our Lord and Savior, be glorified!

May I conclude here, not with my own words, but those of my Lord and Savior, Jesus Christ:

Jesus went through all the towns and villages, teaching in their synagogues, preaching the good news of the Kingdom and healing every disease and sickness. When He saw the crowds, He had compassion on them, because they were harassed and helpless, like sheep without a shepherd. Then He said to His disciples, "The harvest is plentiful but the workers are few. Ask the Lord of the harvest, therefore, to send out workers into His harvest field."

(Matthew 9:35–38, niv1984)

APPENDIX A

My Great Commission

A God leads you to lovingly share *"Three Treasure Chests"* with your own family and friends, perhaps even 30, 60 or 100+ of them in accordance with Jesus' Parable of the Sower, this list is provided for your prayers and convenience. God saw fit to highlight this famous parable in the Holy Bible *three* times for us: in Matthew, Chapter 13; Mark, Chapter 4; and Luke, Chapter 8. It is also conveniently quoted for you in context in its entirety at page 92 of this book. As you meditate on this parable, God will bless you and those around you like never before.

Simply list the names of your own family, friends, coworkers, acquaintances, and others below. Pray for them. After you have given them a copy, simply place a check mark, or even a cross or heart by their name. Please continue to pray for them and help them as God leads you.

<u>Name</u>	<u>Comments/Prayers/Status/Dates</u>

☐ 1. _____

☐ 2. _____

☐ 3. _____

☐ 4. _____

☐ 5. _____

☐ 6. _____

☐ 7. _____

☐ 8. _____

☐ 9. _____

☐ 10. _____

☐ 11. _____

☐ 12. _____

☐ 13. _____

☐ 14. _____

☐ 15. _____

☐ 16. _____

☐ 17. _____

☐ 18. _____

☐ 19. _____

☐ 20. _____

☐ 21. _____

☐ 22. _____

☐ 22. _____

☐ 23. _____

☐ 24. _____

☐ 25. _____

☐ 26. _____

☐ 27. _____

<u>Name</u>	<u>Comments/Prayers/Status/Dates</u>

☐ 28. _____
☐ 29. _____
☐ 30. _____
☐ 31. _____
☐ 32. _____
☐ 33. _____
☐ 34. _____
☐ 35. _____
☐ 36. _____
☐ 37. _____
☐ 38. _____
☐ 39. _____
☐ 40. _____
☐ 41. _____
☐ 42. _____
☐ 43. _____
☐ 44. _____
☐ 45. _____
☐ 46. _____
☐ 47. _____
☐ 48. _____
☐ 49. _____
☐ 50. _____
☐ 51. _____
☐ 52. _____
☐ 53. _____
☐ 54. _____
☐ 55. _____

<u>Name</u>   <u>Comments/Prayers/Status/Dates</u>

☐ 56. _____

☐ 57. _____

☐ 58. _____

☐ 59. _____

☐ 60. _____

☐ 61. _____

☐ 62. _____

☐ 63. _____

☐ 64. _____

☐ 65. _____

☐ 66. _____

☐ 67. _____

☐ 68. _____

☐ 69. _____

☐ 70. _____

☐ 71. _____

☐ 72. _____

☐ 73. _____

☐ 74. _____

☐ 75. _____

☐ 76. _____

☐ 77. _____

☐ 78. _____

☐ 79. _____

☐ 80. _____

☐ 81. _____

☐ 82. _____

☐ 83. _____

Name   Comments/Prayers/Status/Dates

☐ 84. _____
☐ 85. _____
☐ 86. _____
☐ 87. _____
☐ 88. _____
☐ 89. _____
☐ 90. _____
☐ 91. _____
☐ 92. _____
☐ 93. _____
☐ 94. _____
☐ 95. _____
☐ 96. _____
☐ 97. _____
☐ 98. _____
☐ 99. _____
☐ 100+. _____

"I can do all things through Christ which strengtheneth me." Philippians 4:13 (KJV). You can do this. God will help you, strengthen you, and bless you.

Jesus commanded all of us to, "Therefore, go and make disciples of *all* nations, baptizing them in the name of the Father and of the Son and of the Holy Spirit, and teaching them to obey everything I have commanded you. And surely I am with you always, to the very end of the age." Matthew 28:19-20.

Jesus commanded *every* Christian to witness to others both near and far, "And you will be my witnesses in Jerusalem, and in all Judea and Samaria, and to the ends of the earth." Acts 1:8.

Paul set a great example for us by passionately and effectively telling others, especially his own family and friends, the good news of Jesus Christ "in the hope that I may somehow arouse my own people to envy and save some of them." Romans 11:14.

To every friend you would give a free mansion on Earth, offer them an eternal mansion in Heaven.

To every friend you would lovingly and immediately warn of an approaching deadly wildfire on Earth, please lovingly warn them of the eternal flames of Hell.

To God be the glory.

About the Author of
Three Treasure Chests

Mitchell Newport grew up working hard on his family's large Angus cattle ranch near Stratford, Oklahoma. He is a graduate of East Central University with a bachelor of science degree in environmental science; a graduate of the United States Air Force Air Command and Staff College (masters level curriculum in military leadership and management); and alumni of the University of Oklahoma Law School with a Juris doctorate degree in law. He has also extensively studied, written about, and personally developed and taught numerous in depth Bible studies and multimedia seminars over the past thirty years about many aspects of Christian theology while he and his devoted wife served God in many other capacities as active members of the First Baptist Church in Ada, Oklahoma, and most recently at Crossway First Baptist Church in Sulphur.

Mitchell served as a commissioned officer in the United States Air Force for over twenty-five years and retired in the grade of Lieutenant Colonel. He is a veteran of the 1991 Persian Gulf War, the Kosovo Conflict, the War in Afghanistan, the 2003 War in

Iraq, and the Global War on Terror. He has provided valuable legal support to numerous major military operations as an Air Force JAG attorney since 1989 and has served special tours to various higher level Air Force headquarters across America and in foreign countries many times. The Air Force individually mobilized Mitchell several times a year at the apex of his career, sending him to Europe for a diverse range of various JAG projects of international scope as an experienced courtroom litigator, including legal support to the US Air Force, other military branches, and the North Atlantic Treaty Organization (NATO).

Mitchell has also served as a special assistant United States attorney for the Department of Justice, an Oklahoma Supreme Court certified mediator, and several years as president of a nationwide environmental consulting firm. He has traveled extensively throughout America and to dozens of foreign countries. He is a fascinating teacher, lecturer, and author who has previously served as an expert witness and even provided key joint congressional testimony on behalf of the US military and complex environmental remediation projects. Many more fascinating details illuminate this accomplished author. They provide compelling perspectives to this uniquely dynamic book and concept that is saving souls, transforming America, and literally changing the world for the better.

Mitchell lives in southern Oklahoma with two angels: his wife, Darla and daughter, Mikayla. Their amazing Christian Faith, love and support continually remind him, inspire him, and compel him to lovingly share Jesus with every soul he truly cares about and dynamically help others do the same for their own family and friends.

Have a Blessed day! †

Mitchell Newport

mitchell.newport3tc@gmail.com

P.S. People's final words are often very meaningful. After I depart for Heaven, I would like my heartfelt words and thoughts in *Three Treasure Chests* to be my loving legacy to others and to all of my loved ones. To God be the glory. God's will, not mine, be done. Amen.